HERMAPHRODITES, GYNOMORPHS AND JESUS

She-Male Gods
and
the Roots of Christianity

by Dr. David Hillman

HERMAPHRODITES, GYNOMORPHS AND JESUS

She-Male Gods
and
the Roots of Christianity

by Dr. David Hillman

RONIN

Hermaphrodites, Gynomorphs and Jesus

Copyright 2013: D.C.A. Hillman
ISBN: 978-1-57951-171-5

Published by
Ronin Publishing, Inc.
PO Box 3008
Oakland, CA 94609
www.roninpub.com

Credits:

    Illustrations from Clipart.com

    Cover: Hellenistic statue of Hermaphroditus: marble copy of a fresco from Herculaneum. Artist unknown.

Production:

    Cover & Book Design: Beverly A. Potter.
    Editor: Mark J. Estren, Ph.D.

Library of Congress Card Number: 2013945846
Distributed to the book trade by PGW/Perseus

DEDICATION

For the Order of the Rose.

OTHER BOOKS

by Dr. David Hillman

The Chemical Muse
Drug Use and the Roots of Western Civilization

Original Sin
Ritual Child Rape & the Church

TABLE OF CONTENTS

INTRODUCTION

Religion is a wormhole; it is a multidimensional, collapsible bridge in space that only a thirteen-year-old girl in the bloom of life can open... and only when she has entered a state of heightened sexual arousal. According to ancient Etruscan sibyls, the teenage priestesses who established the norms for much of Roman culture, religion is a method of cosmic tunneling; it's a practice that creates a fluid structure through which dark-matter-breathing beings can travel in order to possess their maddened devotees. The ancient world believed religion was a resonant span across the fabric of space-time; and ancient clerics taught that its thermodynamic seal could be forcefully broken open with the songs of maidens.

The Bloom

The Romans spoke classical Latin. Their word "religio," from which

In the Greco-Roman way of thinking, gods are the cosmic bloom of existence. we derive our English word "religion," means "ligature" or "binding." Modern historians, overly influenced by their own Christian cultural lens, have interpreted this to mean religion is something that binds us to do and say certain things in celebration of divinity; in other words, religion is what we owe the gods. Nothing could be further from the historical actuality. In Rome, "religio" was simply the cosmic tie that bound the Earth-plane to the rest of the multiverse. It was a means to an end; it was a force of extra-dimensional attraction.

The Importance of Demons

The ancient Mediterranean world taught that priestesses, witches, diviners and poets possessed the ability to open portals through which sentient powers or "demons" who inhabited extra-worldly planes could travel to the material universe. These beings, these powers-that-be, did not have a physical form; they were not composed of "atoms," the indivisible elements of our world, and they did not have eyes, ears, mouths, voices, or, in fact, any human or biological attributes at all. And perhaps most importantly, these immortals were neither male nor female; they were neither, and yet they were both.

In the Greco-Roman way of thinking, gods are the cosmic bloom of existence. Greek and Latin culture, preserved in the amber of ancient literature, perpetuated the view that gods are the immortal "elements" of an ordered and living universe. For example, Aphrodite is the desire of sexual attraction; Dionysus is ecstasy; Athena is civic justice. Unlike humans, the gods aren't born, they don't age, and they don't die. They are in perpetual bloom.

Myth was the medium in which the classical world expressed the efflorescence of the immortal forces of the universe. Greek and Roman myth had an extraordinary influence on ancient artists, statesmen, religious leaders and philosophers. It was a cultural cement that facilitated the construction of democracy, the establishment of education, and the creation of the scientific method. Ancient myth was a metaphor for expressing the individuality and actions of the immortal powers that govern the universe.

Geometry and Myth

For the Greeks, pioneers of the study of geometry, circles, squares and triangles were no different from myths. They did not exist in reality; you can't touch a circle or hold one in the palm of your hand—shapes are just conceptual representations of mathematical realities. In the same way, the Greeks viewed stories of male and female gods who walked among mortals and interacted with them as nothing less than a means of expressing immaterial reality. The fact that you can't see a circle unless you

The gender of the gods was recognized in antiquity as a means of relating the confounding realities of non-physical cosmic forces.

draw one does not make it any less real. The ancient world believed the same principle applied to gods and demons.

Like circles and squares, the gods—the immortal visitors from other dimensions—had concrete shapes. They assumed certain personalities and characteristics. Hades, king of the dead, was unrelenting and unforgiving; Zeus, ruler of the ordered universe, was known for his foresight; Poseidon, master of the oceanic waters of change, was irritable and ready to cause great earthquakes at a moment's notice. Mother Nature, goddess of generation, was characterized by her power to both nourish and destroy living things.

The "he" and "she" or gender of the gods was recognized in antiquity as a means of relating the confounding realities of non-physical cosmic forces. Contrary to modern feminism and classical scholarship, there was never an ancient religious war between matriarchy and patriarchy, because the Greeks and Romans taught that

Pan

gods do not have actual genders—just as they don't
wear sandals, eat lunch, or braid their hair. Gender was
an "angle" in the pictorial representation of the gods.
Athena was feminine, because she was the nourishing force of civic justice. Pan, the divine shepherd of
nymphs, was masculine because his fear-inducing sex-
drive was responsible for maintaining the frenzied flight
of nature's procreative sprits; the word "panic," taken
from his name, expressed the fear of a young girl walking by herself in a forest.

Gender in myth was a means of expressing immortal, cosmic reality; no Greeks or Romans ever believed
their gods had actual vaginas or penises. Sometimes a
god is male; other times she is
female; and sometimes the same Gynomorphs
god is a he-she, a being of both   formed a
a masculine and a feminine na-   bridge between
ture. Again, this is difficult for   the sexes.
a modern audience to compre-
hend when it has traditionally divided ancient deities
into "gods" and "goddesses." However, the ancient reality is far different. There were no gods and goddesses in
antiquity; there were just cosmic, ageless beings with
masculine, feminine and sometimes bi-gendered traits.

The Bi-Gendered God

The "gynomorph" was a bi-gendered god with both
masculine and feminine attributes. The word itself is
just a pairing of gyno- "woman" with morph- "shape."
Literally, a gynomorph is a god with female-like shape.
Traditionally, the gynomorph was a developed or evolved

state of a feminine divinity or "daimon" (demon in English). Gynomorphs were portrayed as effeminate young males, like Dionysus, a masculine god who possessed distinctly feminine features. Gynomorphs retained the creative capacity of female divinities—they had cosmic wombs—but they also possessed the inseminating abilities attributed to more-masculine gods.

Gynomorphs were special because they stood in the gender-gap between male and female gods. Gynomorphs formed a bridge between the sexes. They were a combination, or the sum, of both genders. In this way, gynomorphs were hermaphroditic, and could appear sometimes as predominantly masculine, and other times as predominantly feminine.

The gynomorph was an important figure in ancient culture because the Greco-Roman world possessed no word for "gender." They viewed sex not as a binary proposition, but as a natural sum of two cooperative potentials; that is, masculinity and femininity were measurements of a sexual scale. In their view, sexual attributes were a combination of both zmasculine and feminine qualities. There were no absolutes; sexual characteristics were combinations of gender. For this reason, their closest word to English "gender" was "kind."

The early Church adapted and intentionally borrowed elements of pagan mystery cults.

Purification

Early Church fathers, bishops and priests were very concerned with issues of divine sexuality and gender.

Ancient mystery religions were deeply concerned with the ideas of masculinity, femininity and hermaphroditism. Greek and Roman cults focused on a process of ritual initiation, during which newcomers were put through a rigorous purification. This cleansing enabled new acolytes to learn the secrets of the particular mystery cults into which they were being initiated, while preparing them for the reception of the special mystic knowledge embodied in the cult myth.

The mystery religions that celebrated the gods Cybele, Isis and Dionysus were particularly prominent in Roman society, especially during the rise of Christianity. As the early Church developed, it absorbed, adapted and intentionally borrowed elements of pagan mystery cults while simultaneously struggling to achieve its own independent status. Early Christians did not want to be mistaken for pagan mystery worshippers, but much of Christianity arose from the practices held in common with these prominent pagan cults. As a result, early Church fathers, bishops and priests were very concerned with issues of divine sexuality and gender.

The classical world was very much concerned with the mystic union of the sexes and even promoted the west's first same-sex marriages. Ancient authors reveal much about the sexual practices surrounding marriage and the marriage celebration; for example, it was cus-

R aising the dead was a well-established ritual by the time Jesus entered the stage of western history.

tomary for virgins intimidated by the proposition of vaginal intercourse to offer anal intercourse on the night of their nuptials as a substitute. This was not considered odd by the ancient world, but was in fact a mainstream sexual practice due to the fact that anal intercourse did not hold the rigorous taboo perpetuated by the Christian world. In fact, many ancient medicines were administered anally after being rubbed onto dildos, and some priestesses even practiced a form of "sacred sodomy" on their devotees.

Anal and vaginal intercourse were valued in antiquity as additional or supplemental means of accessing the divine. Ancient witches and priestesses of Priapus—the god with the constant erection—performed necromantic rituals involving the use of dildos and drugs that were meant to open portals to Erebus, the dimensional plane known as the underworld. This form of ancient "religio," or religion, was perhaps the earliest type of western worship; its roots can be found in the very oldest Roman religious practices, particularly in the cult activities of the Etruscans, the Italic tribe living north of the city of Rome that laid the foundations for all of Roman religion. The figure of the gynomorph was central to the myths and practices of Etruscan and Roman necromancers.

Origins of Necromancy

T he earliest origins of western necromancy are found
in the practices of Etruscan priestesses and prophets.
These "vates," or seers, were able to divine the future
based on their reading of natural signs. They believed
cosmic intelligences freely communicated with mortals, and they taught that the proper interpretation of
signs—like lightning strikes and the flight of birds—was
the provenance of specialized clerics. These same clerics
worshipped gynomorphic gods and perpetuated myths
of bi-gendered, divine entities.

Necromancy was extremely popular during the birth
and early development of Christianity. Raising the dead
was a common practice of Roman and Greek religious
figures and was a well-established ritual by the time
Jesus entered the stage of western history. Necromancers
performed sacred sexual acts meant to summon and drive
out demons from the afflicted. The highest aspiration
of any ancient necromancer was the resurrection of the
dead; this enabled practitioners of the dark arts to deter-
mine the future and to derive prophetic vision. Christianity developed under the influence of these necromantic rituals and openly advanced the very same practices.

The purpose of ancient western religion was to open
a means of communication with the realms of the gods.
Classical necromancers practiced their religion by opening
portals to the kingdom of the dead. The oldest sibyls—the
earliest western prophets—taught that the resurrection or
summoning of the gods from the underworld was a necessary step in restoring justice to the universe.

For necromancers, the gynomorph was the key to restoring the bloom of universal justice, something that could only be enforced by the gods. The bi-gendered gynomorph became the ultimate resurrection-savior of humanity. The gynomorph was a goddess-with-a-penis who became the most important figure of all ancient religion...including both paganism and Christianity.

1:

SEXUAL TRANSFORMATIONS

"Oldest of the prophets, she lifts her hands to the heavens and prays to receive a penis."

—PRIAPEIA

There is no word for "gender" in either Latin or Greek. Not surprisingly, these same ancient languages also lack vocabulary for terms like "homosexual," "heterosexual" and even "sexuality" it-self. The closest the Romans and Greeks ever got to the modern concept of gender was a word for the sexes best translated by the English "offspring" or "kind." There is no word for gender in classical antiquity because pre-Christian Europe viewed sexuality as a cycle, not an immutable state of being.

What is Gender?

When the Greeks and Romans talked about sex, they did so in three dimensions. As polytheists who worshipped both masculine and feminine divinities, they were unbound by the restrictive principles of monotheistic systems like those employed by Judaism and Christianity.

Monotheism, unlike polytheism, favors one gender over another.

When it comes to sexuality, monotheism is strictly binary; polytheism bends both ways. For example, according to Moses, every human and animal is born either male or female; the cosmos is monotone and the natural world is black and white. In contrast, the classical world believed masculinity and femininity were gradations of a geometric scale; as pagan natural scientists and philosophers readily admitted, some animals are born male, some female, some with both sexes, some with neither...and some species could even change with time.

Monotheism, unlike polytheism, also favors one gender over another. In the eyes of Jewish, Christian and Muslim holy men, wisdom was something handed down to masculine mortals by a masculine god. Greeks and Romans thought differently. From the perspective of the priests and poets who created western civilization, the greatest prophet of the Mediterranean world was a guy named Teiresias; and he was a blind man whose incredible visionary abilities derived from his life experiences as both a man and a woman.

Teiresias gained his divine perspective through becoming both genders. As an adult, he was magically transformed into a woman. According to Ovid, who was arguably the greatest Roman love poet, Teiresias gained incredible insight through his particular transgender metamorphosis. The seer's reputation as the world's greatest prophet was the direct result of his experiences as both male and female.

Teiresias' prophetic foresight was a divine gift. Jupiter, the king of heaven, gave him this boon in order to balance the curse of his Olympian wife, Juno. Teiresias, because of his peculiar ability to understand the world as both a man and a woman, once solved a dispute between the king and queen of heaven over who enjoys sex more—men or women. When the divine royals consulted Teiresias on the subject, he proclaimed that women experience nine-tenths of all sexual pleasure while men only feel a meager tenth of the fun. For revealing this secret Juno struck the poor prophet with blindness; in gratitude for his honesty, Jupiter tenderly compensated his loss.

As Ovid put it in his *Metamorphoses*, "The all-powerful father of the gods, in order to balance Teiresias' ocular castration, gave him the ability to know the future, and thus lightened his punishment with great honor."

Teiresias possessed a unique awareness of the experience of both genders and thus possessed a deeper-than-average awareness of the divine machinery of the cosmos. And this meant that transgender beings were the wisest of all mortals.

GREEK YOUTH

Both Male & Female

In the Greek mind, it was not difficult to be simultaneously male and female. Adonis, the lover of
Aphrodite-Urania, the Syrian queen of life, was himself
both a boy and a girl. According to the *Orphic Hymns*,
a collection of writings whose content was universally
attributed to the Thracian poet Orpheus, Adonis was
both a young unmarried girl or *kore* and a post-pubes-
cent teenage boy or *koros*.

It makes good sense that Adonis was worshipped as
both male and female. For, as the lover of Aphrodite-
Urania, he was the object of affection of the great goddess of desire, whose seductively feminine statues sometimes sported their own large erect penises. Herodotus,
the famed Greek historian, called this bisexual Aphrodite by the name Mithra, and equated her worship with
the Persian celebration of Mithras, an eastern god with
both masculine and feminine characteristics.

The Athenians celebrated a manifestation of this
two-sexed lover of Adonis and called her by the name
Aphroditus. In order to honor the establishment of
this cult, men and women routinely exchanged clothing and assumed alternate sexual roles. Our ancient
sources even make it sound as if women assumed a
penetrative role while men celebrated the passive sexual experience. This wouldn't be odd for antiquity; we know that witches

The temples and groves of Aphrodite and Priapus used sexual activity as a means of medicating the public.

and priestesses routinely sexually penetrated the devotees of specific gods (see Chapter 7).

Cults that cel-ebrated "Aphrodite of the Garden" employed statues of "Aphroditus," which were nothing more or less than simple phallic sculptures. In this way, the word "Aphroditus" came to represent an upright, stone representation of a penis, similar to the famous Herms of antiquity, which were quadrangular columns topped with the head of the god Hermes and adorned with a prominent penis.

Earth effortlessly
        crafted a reaper,
    the cosmic birth of
sexuality from an eternal,
    immutable past.
                —HESIOD,
            THEOGONY

Guardians of the Garden

Cults of a masculine, penetrative Aphrodite were invaluable in the ancient world. As in the worship of Priapus by Roman witches, these "guardians of the garden" facilitated the practice of ancient medicine and gynecology. Priests and priestesses, acting as local physi-cians and midwives, used dildos made of various materi-als in order to apply drugs both vaginally and anally.

Lacking the technology for sterile intramuscular injection, the Greeks and Romans recognized that nu-merous pharmaceuticals were best applied through the tissues of the rectum and the vagina. Drugs compound-ed with oil bases were applied to sacred dildos and then introduced into these portals. In this way, priests and witches were able to perform magical ceremonies cel-

Hermaphroditic gods and divine castration were not ignored by the early Church fathers. ebrating the penetrative god of the garden while using potent botanicals to effect medical cures.

Just as Apollo was worshipped as the great oracular god of healing at various shrines throughout the ancient world, where priestesses gave more advice on medicine than any other single topic, temples and groves of Aphrodite and Priapus used sexual activity as a means of medicating the public.

Both Aphrodite and Priapus were associated with the image of castration. In traditional Greek religion, the daughter of Uranus was born when her father's erect penis was violently cut from his body as he readied himself for intercourse with his consort Gaia. His genitalia were thrown into the sea, and the milky white semen that spewed from them produced the goddess herself—by name Aphrodite-Urania.

The Uranian image of emasculation was preserved in the statues and myth of Priapus, who was often prominently featured as holding his monstrously large erection in his left hand and a sickle in his right.

The Sickle

The "sickle" with which the penis and testicles were removed from Uranus—the reaping instrument used for the generation of the female form of Aphrodite—was called an unbreakable "genos," the very same word used by the Greeks to indicate "offspring," "kind" or "sex."

In this way the ancient world taught that sexual identity was a process of creative castration and that the sexes were not made as separate natural entities but developed from each other; Aphrodite-Urania, the beautiful female goddess, was a transgendered Uranus. She, like Priapus, stood ready with the great reaper to change her divine masculine form into the divine feminine.

Of course, castration was only the beginning of the sexual cycle for the Greeks and Romans. Their ancient pantheons are built upon the cyclical, sexual transformation of divinity.

There are three stages to the sexual metamorphoses of Greco-Roman gods. First a bi-gendered primordial divinity comes into being—marking the beginning of time. These gods usually represent the basic "elements" or building blocks of the universe. Next, these she-male gods are castrated, an act that gives rise to female creator-goddesses like Aphrodite. These creator goddesses then give birth to living creatures, and the cosmic drama proceeds when they regrow their penis. As the goddess does so, she is transformed into a masculine savior. And finally the cycle is complete when this feminine goddess with a penis—known as a "gynomorph"—establishes cosmic justice.

> The Mother "comes to the man and entrusts her children to his wisdom and his moral uprightness...he unhesitatingly invited the girl to experience sacred sodomy."
> —PETRONIUS, SATYRICON

From Paganism to Christianity

It is very important to understand that the views of the Greeks and Romans in the early centuries of the Church had a significant impact on the practice of Christianity. Jesus, his disciples, and the earliest Christians did not live in a vacuum; the bi-gendered creator gods of their pagan neighbors had a tremendous influence on their own religion, and hence the development of the Christian west.

Hermaphroditic gods and divine castration were not ignored by the early Church fathers. For example, why does the earliest iconography of the Church portray Jesus as a crucified man with an ass's head, an animal typically associated with Dionysus and Priapus? And why did early Christians put stock in Roman sibyls who prophesied the rise of a hermaphroditic Messiah? There may be no clear answers to questions like this, but they do reveal the extent to which pagan views of sexuality influenced the development of western civilization under Christianity.

The figure of Jesus as an ass-headed god was a serious consideration in the early Church. As late as Tertullian, a second-century Church father, a debate existed concerning the prominent belief among Christians that the crucified Jesus was a god with an ass's head. The Church borrowed the image from its pagan neighbors at a time when it was a popular symbol of mystery cults. The worship of Priapus was associated with the sacrifice of an ass, and asses played substantial roles in myths associated with mystery cults.

Sexuality and Jesus

S exuality was not absent from the earliest accounts of the life and mission of Jesus. The gospel of Mark reports the presence of a naked boy with Jesus in the Garden of Gethsemane and discusses the problems Jesus encountered with both his followers and outsiders who were attempting to "scandalize" his association with children. Jesus explained the rationale for his close contact with children when the apostles censured a group of women for bringing their children to Jesus to be "touched." The verb for "touching" here is a Greek word also meaning "to engage a person in a sexual manner." And Jesus' defense of his physical contact with these children borders on the romantic. In fact, the text states that Jesus praised the children only after he applied his hands to them. That is, he embraced the children, touched them—using the word for sexual touch—and then affectionately praised them.

The very same activity Jesus engaged in can be observed in a Roman novel by Petronius called *Satyricon*. In this first-century work, roughly contemporary with the end of Jesus' life and the beginning of Paul's ministry, Petronius describes an episode in which a Roman woman brings her youthful children to an older, wise philosopher with a reputation for moral sobriety. She leaves her kids with the gentleman, who, against the background of the sacred worship of Priapus, proceeds to engage in "sacred sodomy" with them.

Within the context of the transformative property of sexuality valued by first-century mystery cults, the

scene makes more sense. The children in the arms of
the holy philosopher were initiated into the mysteries of sexuality and therefore were transformed by his
blessings. The entire episode is strikingly similar to its
biblical counterpart, with the single exception that
in Petronius' version there are no disciples present to
upbraid the woman for leaving her children with the
master. And of course the Satyricon is framed by the
activities of the priestesses of Priapus.

Gods of Castration

P riapus was the transformative phallic god who sported the gender-bending reaper. As the early Church
struggled for its own identity in the midst of competing
mystery religions that taught a transformative sexuality,
it is not strange that Christians began associating Jesus
with gods of castration. Not only did Jesus employ the
same sex drugs used by these Greek and Roman cults,
but he also used the very same language and ceremony
as it appears in contemporary classical literature. And
what is perhaps most telling is that his enemies—the
religious Jews—claimed he was performing the very
same acts as the demon-manipulating priestesses of
Aphroditus and Priapus.

Greek and Roman views of sexuality set the stage
for the development of western civilization. Gender, in
the Greco-Roman way of thinking, was not sexual identity; gender was a catalyst for transformation. Ancient
religious practices, perpetuated most actively by the
followers of Orpheus and Pythagoras, show us that the

founders of western civilization looked at masculinity and femininity as mathematical concepts with peculiar geometric relationships.

In the ancient Mediterranean, "male" and "female" acted as two sides of a dynamic right triangle. The square of the hypotenuse of this gender triangle was equal to the sum of the squares of its masculine and feminine sides—that is, the Pythagorean hypotenuse was the "gynomorph," a masculine god with feminine creative capacity; magnified by its own image, as if in a mirror, the gynomorph became the totality of the magnification of both genders. Masculine and feminine w e r e   not bio-linguistic absolutes in the minds of t h e   founders of western civilization; they w e r e   simply words that de- fined an intercon- nected sexual real- ity. This was the world encountered by Jesus and his followers; this was the world they adapted and transformed.

2:

SELF-CASTRATION

*"God is both day and night…She changes herself
as does the fire when it combines with incense
to create a new sweet smell."*

—HERACLEITUS

One of early Christianity's biggest competitors was the mystery cult of Cybele and Attis. The Greeks called Cybele, an eastern goddess, by the name of Rhea and openly acknowledged that her worship sprang up in Asia Minor and was closely associated with the frenzied oracular worship of the Thracian Dionysus known as Zagreus. Cybele was followed by a crazed retinue of self-castrating devotees made famous for one very important reason: castration enabled them to join in mystical union with their god.

Divine Mother

During the opening decades of the Roman imperial period, when the students of Jesus still called themselves followers of "the Way" and worshipped in secrecy, much of the western world actively venerated a sacred mother goddess and her young male lover-companion. Much like Aphrodite and Adonis, Cybele and Attis shared their worship as the conjoined manifestation of a motherly force of

Cybele was followed by a crazed retinue of self-castrating devotees.

generation and the cosmic masculine seed required for initiating new life and growth.

Male followers of Cybele, known as Galli, ritually castrated themselves and assumed female attire and habits. Female attendants who acted as the cult's priestesses and prophets intoxicated themselves with mind-altering botanicals and famously stood in prominent public spaces railing against passersby for their impious, hubristic lifestyles that were out of sync with the ethereal realm of the gods.

Before this great Mother goddess was called Cybele by the Phrygians in Asia Minor, her name was Agdistis and she was not a she...but a he/she. Pausanias, a Greek travel writer in the second century of the Common Era, reported the Phrygian myth that Agdistis was a child of the goddess Earth and that he was a hermaphrodite born with both sets of genitalia. Fearing the overwhelming power of this dual-sexed divinity, the other gods castrated

CYBELE

Agdistis—making him into a female—and then buried his male genitalia. From his lost penis sprang a beautiful male god known as Attis.

Lovers Reunited

Of course, we know that Cybele and Attis were eventually reunited as lovers, so how did ancient poets and priests explain what happened to the newly gender-reassigned Agdistis? It's simple: after losing his penis, he became purely female and fell in love with Attis—the seed of his own dismembered sexual organ. And since Agdistis was changed into a woman—who assumed the name Cybele—he...or she...was free to join herself physically with the boy Attis.

Cybele transferred her priesthood to Attis and made the boy agree to sacrifice his own penis should he ever be unfaithful. Unfortunately Attis was seduced by the allure of a river nymph and violently cut off his own genitalia after being driven mad by jealous Cybele. The Galli, eunuch boy-priests of the goddess, actually reenacted this myth when they publicly castrated themselves during festivals celebrating Cybele and Attis. Lucian vividly portrayed the ritual in his *On the Syrian Goddess:*

> "As the Galli sing and celebrate their orgies, frenzy falls on many of them and many who had come as mere spectators afterwards are found to have committed the great act...any young man who has resolved on this action, strips off his clothes, and with a loud shout bursts into the crowd, and picks up a sword...he takes it and castrates himself and then runs wildly through the city, bearing in his hands what he has cut off."

The castrated Galli were a bit of a cultural shock to the Greco-Roman world, but both civilizations eventually embraced the ideals behind this ritual castration. The Romans even went so far as to import the worship of Cybele to Rome. The adoption of her veneration was uncomfortably accompanied by the uncharacteristically Roman goings-on of the Galli and the oracular priestesses of the Mother goddess. However, despite the cultural differences—the Romans had not traditionally embraced the performance of ecstatic self-castration—the Roman world piously adopted the goddess and actively promoted her mystery rituals.

The Galli publicly castrated themselves during festivals celebrating Cybele and Attis.

Ecstasy and Phrygian Christians

In the late third century BCE, as Rome's second war with Carthage raged, Italy perceived the adoption of Cybele's gender-reassigning worship to be a necessary step in defeating the enemies of the Republic. In fact, both the Roman sibyls and the oracle at Delphi directly endorsed the importation of Cybele's worship into Rome as an answer to problems associated with the Second Punic War. As a result, Cybele was brought into Roman religious life and newly minted in Latin as "Magna Mater" or "the Great Mother."

The widespread popularity of the mysteries of Cybele and Attis assured that the cult would eventually come into conflict with Christianity. By the end of the second century CE, a group of Christians in Phrygia, following a man named Montanus and his two female associates, created a break-away sect characterized by its experiences with ecstatic possession. These Montanists, as they came to be known, taught that frenzied, prophetic worship, like that practiced by Cybele's Galli, was the only proper means of celebrating the Christian god.

> The Montanists said that Jesus visited them in the form of a woman.

The Montanists even went so far as to declare that Jesus visited them in the form of a woman. This castrated savior figure was not as far-fetched as Christians from Rome and Alexandria wanted their followers to believe. Some early church fathers heartily embraced the Phrygian movement, and powerful intellectual Christians, up to and including Tertullian himself, promoted the ecstatic teachings of the Montanists. After all, Phrygian Christians were simply following the model already established by their castrated Agdistis, who was himself, as a female, the voice of prophetic ecstasy.

Even later Christians like St. Ambrose, the archbishop of Milan, embraced the image of a feminized or dual-gendered Jesus. In an approach reminiscent of the relationship between Cybele and Attis, leaders of the church presented themselves as the brides of Christ—and often used explicitly sexual language to represent the loving relationship of Christ with his followers. Ambrose even went so far as to extol the nourishment provided by the milky breasts of the Lord and the life-giving womb the Messiah possessed.

Eunuchs for Christ

Cybele's sexual relationship with Attis could not be smothered by the Christian world. The image of the Mother goddess castrating herself in order to create a follower with whom she could mate was far too compelling for the men who made up the intellectual backbone of the early Church. Christians like the Montanists found the image of Cybele's maddening ecstasy a convincing source of inspiration. They were also impressed by the devotion of her priests, who considered their personal dedication to the goddess to be more important than the preservation of their own sex organs.

The overt sexuality of the Phrygian goddess permeated the teachings of the very first   Christians. The most vocal advocate of an openly sexual Jesus was Origen, an Alexandrian Christian and prominent theologian, who embraced a Greek ideal of the Messiah and was eventually condemned as a heretic for his mystic, philosophical teachings.

Most importantly, in the introduction to his commentary on the *Song of Solomon*, Origen

ORIGEN

established an openly sexual aspect of the relationship between the Judeo-Christian god and his followers. Origen used the text of the *Song of Solomon*, a Jewish book about erotic love, to convince his contemporaries that the relationship of the Church to its Messiah was no less of an intimately physical conjoining of two entities than the relationship of Solomon to his historical lover.

Origen's Purification

As in the mysteries of Cybele and Attis, Origen promotes a "purification" ritual in which the followers of Christ are completely purged of a desire for anything other than intimacy with Jesus; this purgation amounted to nothing less than a spiritual, Christian castration. Furthermore, Origen presents Jesus in the vein of the emasculated Agdistis, whose love for the juvenile Attis was an exact reflection of Christ's love for the Church. And in doing so, he sets forth physical castration as a model for believers—using Ignatius as a model, Origen asserts in his *Song of Songs* commentary that the sexual instinct for anything other than Jesus must be "crucified," for, in his mind, boys naturally gravitate toward sexual promiscuity:

> *"For everyone who comes to the age of puberty loves something, whether less than rightly when he loves what he should not, or rightly and beneficially when he loves what he should."*

Like Attis, the young boy representing the Church is ritually castrated in order to ensure fidelity—an almost exact replaying of the theme of devotion embraced by the self-castrating Galli. Origen presents the castrated boy-Church as the new bride of Christ; and she, like a young bride on her wedding night, is "now ready to receive manly power and perfect mystery."

Origen's mystical teachings may have gotten him posthumously excommunicated, but they are in direct alignment with the mystical teachings of ancient mystery religions. In perfect step with the Phrygian cult of Cybele and Attis, the Christians taught that the ecstasy of religious communion with the all-powerful god was only possible when devotees were purged of their sexual capacity by means of spiritual castration.

For Cybele as for Jesus, the loss of masculinity by means of self-sacrifice was a way of joining oneself with god. Cybele and Attis together were Agdistis, just as the crucified Jesus wedded to his Church became a single, all powerful, dual-gendered son of God.

And for anyone who might want to question Origen's commitment to the power of the purification ritual performed by Phrygian eunuch priests of Cybele, it is important to remember that Origen, in a reported ecstatic frenzy, cut off his own genitalia.

Everyone who comes to the age of puberty loves something.

—ORIGEN

3:

ANCIENT SAME-SEX MARRIAGE

"Why do you come to this sacred wedding, Juno, guide of brides? Why do you come, Hymen, where we who marry are both girls?"

—OVID

Neutering oneself for love is easy; the Galli, servants of Cybele, readily forsook their masculinity for a chance to be joined to their castrated god, very much as the Christian theologian Origen cut his own penis off to be closer to Christ. But what about women? Can one woman possess another? Is it possible for a female to satisfy a burning desire to penetrate a fellow female lover? According to the founders of democracy, it's not only possible, it's Nature's most sincere expression of desire.

Female Love

Ovid narrates the story of a same-sex love affair that ended up happily in the bonds of sacred matrimony. Iphis was a beautiful boy...or so her father thought. When she was born, her mother hid the fact that she wasn't a boy by isolating her and by giving her a gender-nonspecific name: the Greek name Iphis is like modern-day "Alex" or "Kerry," a name that ancient parents gave to both boys and girls.

Why did Iphis have to hide her gender? Because her father made clear that his wife was to eliminate their newborn if it happened to be born without a penis. However, thankfully for Iphis, several Egyptian divinities appeared to her pregnant mother in a dream and ordered her to disregard her husband's cruel demand and embrace her soon-to-be-born daughter. She gladly complied with the wishes of the gods, and in order to avoid the wrath of her husband, raised her girl as if she were a boy.

In order to avoid the wrath of her husband, Iphis' mother raised her girl as if she were a boy.

When Iphis was a child, her natural beauty was overwhelming, but at the same time completely indiscernible from the physical beauty of a pre-pubescent boy:

"Her mother, by means of deceit, successfully perpetuated the pious ruse of her daughter's masculine gender. Iphis was groomed as a boy; her body was beautifully proportioned and could easily pass for that of either a young boy or a young girl."

Of course, when Iphis turned thirteen, problems arose. While Iphis progressed through puberty, her father remained ignorant of her true gender identity and happily arranged her marriage to a beautiful young schoolmate named Ianthe. By a stroke of fate, it happened that Iphis had already fallen madly in love with the girl. However, despite her affection for Ianthe, Iphis knew that her secret would be uncovered on the day of her nuptials and that her father would probably kill her for such an embarrassing deception.

Holy Gender Change

T he myth of Iphis was compelling for the people of
antiquity not because of its girl-on-girl love interest, but because of Iphis' desire to play the part of the
penetrator. By the first century, when Ovid was compos-
ing his poetry, the classical world already embraced the
legitimate reality of lesbian relationships. In fact, our
word "lesbian" is derived from the name for natives of
the Greek island of Lesbos, where the lyric poet Sappho
openly composed erotic poetry for her female paramours.
The word "lesbian" retained a nonsexual meaning until
the 20th century. In the last operetta collaboration between Gilbert and Sullivan, *The Grand Duke*, there is a
chorus praising the delights of "Lesbian wine."

Sappho, the Lesbian, was so respected that Ovid
and his contemporaries considered her to be a divinely
inspired poet and even referred to her as the tenth
Muse. Sappho's sexuality was not an issue; the story of
Iphis was not shocking because of its lesbian leanings,
but because of the desire of its protagonist to take on
the active physical role of the penetrator, something
reserved for the masculine sex.

Modern classicists, due to their reliance on the
monotheistic Christian cultural lens, tend to ignore
overt sexual references of such a scandalous nature, but
the name Iphis itself is as titillating as it is openly pro-
vocative. Related Greek roots, like "phys" and "phit,"
can be translated with the English "to father" and "to
sow" or "to plant." The roots that make up Iphis' name
clearly label her as the inseminator, a role traditionally

reserved for men. And on the flip-side of this lock-in-key sexual mythology, Iphis' lover, Ianthe, derives her name from the word for "flower." In other words, Iphis was the seed-spreading bee and Ianthe was the pollen-receiving bloom.

MYTH-MAKERS

But Ovid is playing a linguistic trick on his audience, and the real significance of the word-play in this myth of metamorphosis is not with the shocking use of penetration for the female sex, but with the little letter "i" that our clever poet affixes to the names of the two lovers. That is, Iphis and Ianthe are not just the "penetrator" and the "bud," but they are a "divinely-inspired" lesbian duo. For the "i" in Greek was used to denote the ecstatic cry rendered in the mantic worship of Greek oracular gods, including Apollo, Cybele and Dionysus.

Ovid goes to great lengths to let his readers know that Io was the goddess who appeared in a dream to Iphis' mother...Io, the maddened heifer, the teenage girl who wandered the Earth in search of a cure for her "oistromanes." And what is "oistromanes"? It is love-madness; a state of insanity caused by the stinging pain of something the Greeks called "oistros," the frenzy-inducing gadfly that accompanies the erotic inspiration of the female spirit at specific times during the menstrual cycle. We derive our English word "estrus"—the period of sexual arousal that precedes ovulation—from the same Greek concept. Io, the goddess who interceded for Iphis, was the goddess of maddening sexual desire.

Ovid uses a well-known Greek play—*Prometheus Bound* by Aeschylus—to explain the tragedy of the soon-to-be-born lesbian Iphis, who herself plays the part of the male aggressor Zeus to the sexually receptive teenage girl. Iphis takes the place of Zeus because he was the notorious lover of young maidens in Greek myth:

> **Chorus**: *"Do you hear the Muse singing through the young girl with the horns?..."*

> **Io:** *"This god-sent disease consumes my body; it thrusts into me and penetrates me with its maddening spear."*

The word for "penetrate" in Aeschylus' play employs the same root as that found in the name Iphis. Stated otherwise, Iphis is the female spear of penetration; Iphis is the female penis.

The Goddess' Penis

B ut how did Iphis complete her transformation? She was already a penetrator in spirit, but as a natural female, she clearly lacked the physical spear of a husband. The solution for such a quandary was simple: since the gods are themselves bi-gendered by nature, they are logically able to fix gender assignment issues.

Io, the Greek goddess who protected Iphis from death by appearing in her mother's dream, was readily recognized in antiquity as the Egyptian goddess Isis. And fortunately for Iphis and her mother, Isis was especially known for her knack for penis replacement. In fact, Isis was the guardian of her own lover's severed penis and appropriately shepherded the great cosmic phallus of creation. Ovid writes that Iphis' mother, knowing Isis' power, took her daughter to a temple of the goddess and begged her for help:

> "Oh Isis…help us, I pray, and heal our sore distress…Tears followed on her words. The goddess seemed to move, nay, moved her altar, the doors of the temple shook…rejoicing in the good omen, the mother left the temple; and Iphis walked beside her as she went, but with a longer stride than was her wont. Her face seemed of a darker hue, her strength seemed greater, her very features sharper…she seemed more vigorous than was her girlish wont. In fact, you who were but lately a girl are now a boy!"

Isis transformed Iphis from a girl into a boy in what appears to be history's first gender reassignment surgery. Iphis is embraced as a genuine boy and the gods openly sanction his marriage to Ianthe:

"Go make your offerings at the shrines; rejoice with
gladness unafraid! They make their offerings at the
shrines and add a votive tablet; the tablet had the
inscription: These gifts as man did Iphis pay which
once as maid he vowed."

It may seem foreign to a modern audience steeped in
the western Christian tradition to accept such a radical
transformation, but the Greeks and Romans sanctioned
the phenomenon of gender transformation on numerous
occasions.

Not surprisingly, the myth of Iphis is just one of
many gender reassignments found in the literature of
antiquity. Among others, Leucippus, another famous
mythological girl, was given a penis by an immortal—in
this case the Greek goddess Leto, whose son was notoriously feminine and whose daughter was notoriously
masculine. The specific example of Leucippus' gender
reassignment was striking because she was so beautiful
as a girl, and the goddess who enabled her transition
was actually celebrated as "The Grafter," an epithet
that indicates the idea of switching genders was more
commonplace than it may seem.

It is fair to say that classical civilization—where
there was no word for "homosexuality" or "gender"—
more openly embraced the mutability of sexual identity.
And curiously, in each gender transformation found in
ancient myth, the outcome is distinctly positive for the
transgendered individual. The process of altering one's
sexual organs was even considered a divinely inspired
movement forward on the path toward enlightenment.

Isis transformed Iphis from a girl into a boy in what appears to be history's first gender reassignment surgery.

Following Isis

Again, this may be disturbing to a 21st-century western world, challenging the long-held beliefs of post-modern Christianity, but even the early followers of Jesus recognized the value of sexual transformation. Gender reassignment may be anathema to modern Catholics and Evangelicals, but early Christians actually followed the example of their pagan neighbors and venerated a hermaphroditic Messiah.

4:

DRUGS, ECSTASY & THE HYMEN

"A virgin is a terrible teacher."

—MARTIAL

J ohn the apostle said, "God is love". And with such profoundly influential words, the apostle of love set a metaphorical fire in the heart of church members that would continue to burn for over two thousand years. As long as the Church held sway in Europe, Christians celebrated their relationship with the Messiah as if it were a love affair between a man and a woman. And in *Ephesians*, Paul was quick to cement the idea of Jesus as bridegroom of his followers by promoting the image of Christ washing his lover with a ritual bath, a sacred rite that preceded ancient weddings.

Cupid's Arrows

F or the Greeks and Romans, the idea of "God is love" was by no means a difficult pill to swallow. Centuries before Jesus lived, the ancient world venerated Eros, a winged boy-god who set sexual passion in the hearts of lovers. Eros, known as Cupid by the Romans, wielded his bow with its passion-inducing arrows in a way that

caused as much harm as it did good, but the proof of
his value as a member of the polytheistic pantheon was
his ability to perpetuate natural life; Eros created all
life forms by means of biological generation. Thanks to
this god of sexual desire—which is what "eros" means
in Greek—humans and animals are able to produce offspring. In short, the Greeks and Romans believed Eros
perpetuated the march of life.

Of course it makes good sense that a messianic
figure should be portrayed as a force of love and protec-
tion, but the association of the Christian god with the
love of marriage was also fraught with peril. It is not obvious to a modern audience, but in antiquity associating
the god of marital passion with Jesus was a striking dec-
laration. For, as the early church readily acknowledged,
Love was a dual-gendered entity. Early Christians had
no problem with the prophecies of Roman sibyls about
the coming of a hermaphroditic Messiah, because the
god Love himself was simultaneously a boy and a girl.

A Frolicsome Gang

Much of the art and literature that dominated classical Greece and Rome is full of images of the
"Erotes." The Erotes were the openly effeminate and
frolicsome gang of young boys who followed Eros and
Aphrodite, spreading sexual desire with their fire-
starting arrows. Before they were pictured as pudgy,
precocious babies, they were depicted as randy, same-
sex-loving teenagers. And prominent among their ranks
was Hymenaeus, the god of the marriage ceremony.

Like other classical deities, Hymenaeus—whom we know simply as Hymen—was worshipped with a shout. The Greek world considered specific passion-induced utterances to be of a religious nature and further believed these vocalizations were an expression of worship. For example, when women who gave birth moaned in triumphal agony during the delivery of their children, the ancient world looked on their shouts as hymns to the goddess of childbirth. When soldiers entered battle, their fear-rousing war-cry was considered an offering to the god of war. And in the same manner, when a Greek or Roman girl consummated her marriage, her shouts of sexual ecstasy were considered to be the veneration of Hymen, the god of the marital union. Carl Orff captured the spirit of this marital religious ecstasy in his cantata called *Trionfo di Afrodite*, whose climax is the shouting, in climax, of a newly wedded woman.

WINGS
OF
DESIRE

Hymen Dressed as a Girl

According to Greek legend, Hymen was so delicately beautiful that he could easily be mistaken for a young girl. Like other followers of Eros, Hymen was playfully effeminate. And the god's malleable gender served him well. For, in one particular myth, Hymen disguised himself as a young girl in order to pursue a lover, and his convincing female disguise ended up saving the girl and her playmates from pirates. The two were eventually married, and the hymn to Hymen became part of the mystery celebration of marriage.

Hymns to Hymen marked the official marriage processions of Greco-Roman antiquity, but the figure of the god Hymen became closely associated with brides in particular. Like the image of the Christian love-God, Hymen came to represent the passion of the bride. Long before women's hymen—the vaginal tissue sometimes torn during the first act of coitus—took its name from the deity, the god Hymen represented the mysterious entry of newly-wedded girls into the world of reproduction, generation and motherhood.

Hymen was the god of the female transition from a non-productive girl to a fecund matriarch. Hymen's hymns and shouts marked the coming of age of womanhood and the origin of life for mortals. And since

Hymns to Hymen marked the official marriage processions of Greco-Roman antiquity.

Hymen represented the bride, he was often depicted as the recipient of sexual advances.

On the night of their first coital union, the Romans held to a tradition that allowed young, scared girls the

Ovid indicates that the first night of the marriage was frequently spent under the influence of pain-killing drugs.

right to substitute anal intercourse for vaginal. Martial, in his *Epigrams*, made this clear:

> *"She will let her eager spouse sodomize her once,*
> *while she fears the first wound of the new lance, but*
> *her nurse and her mother will forbid its happening*
> *often and say: 'She's your wife, not your boy.'"*

A Learning Process

The process of engaging in anal intercourse allowed young Roman brides to learn the dynamics of sexual intercourse before having to suffer the painful prospects of the body's first vaginal penetration. In this way, the Romans viewed the bride as a sort of Hymen figure herself, an effeminate male, willing to participate in anal penetration.

Of course, not all Roman brides were virgins; ancient physicians like Soranus asserted that girls who waited more than a couple of years after puberty to have sex were not of the majority and typically ended up with serious psychological problems. And if the mythic literature can be used to support the opinions of doctors, it is safe to say that teenagers in antiquity regularly engaged in intercourse as a recreational activity outside

of marriage. Nymphs and doctors aside, the ancient
literary standard makes it seem as if young love was far
more the rule than the exception.

Ovid, the Roman love poet, shows us that the first
night of the marriage was frequently spent under the influence of pain-killing drugs. In a passage from his *Fasti*,
a treatise about the Roman calendar, Ovid draws upon
the marriage of Venus and Mars to illustrate the ancient
custom of giving a young bride-to-be a dose of opiates
before the wedding-night festivities:

> *"Without hesitation, go purchase the poppy, carefully
> rubbed for its snow white latex, and honey flowing
> from pressed combs, since Venus herself, when first
> led to her aroused husband, drank this concoction
> and from that time onward was a bride."*

Once again, the association of the effeminate god
Hymen with the bride is informative. Ancient sexual
stimulants were more frequently administered via the
rectum than orally due to the fast rate of drug absorption through the colon. And these drugs were administered, whether orally or rectally, after being applied to
dildos, rods, or the penis. In this way, both the male and
female partners benefited from the drugs.

Hymen's symbolic interest in anal penetration
facilitated the application of the very same drugs that
were given to young girls on the night of their nuptials.
In other words, the Roman use of anal intercourse on
the night of the wedding may have been a practical
means of administering pain-relieving, anxiolytic medicines to young brides. The figure of Hymen dressed as a

girl is important because it shows that the receptivity to anal intercourse was an important step in the marriage ceremony. Hymen, as the representative of the bride, had to be a willing partner and receptive of the act of anal penetration.

Screaming in Ecstasy

Ancient priestesses of Priapus, the Greco-Roman god who protected life's "gardens," regularly used dildos, sacred objects and even statues with erections to apply medicines and to induce altered states of consciousness. Several episodes in Petronius' *Satyricon* aptly illustrate the use of anal intercourse in religion, leisure and medicine. In fact, the Roman world witnessed the invention of numerous potent drug concoctions that were meant to stimulate, facilitate or prohibit sexual activity. And many of these strong drugs were applied to rectal tissues through the act of anal intercourse.

The shouts of young brides on the night of their coital union with their new husbands were represented by ecstatic songs about Hymen performed by the marriage processions found in weddings of Greeks and Romans. These songs symbolized the mystery initiation of young brides engaging in intercourse on the night of their wedding, and as such were not lost on the Christian world.

> Many strong drugs were applied to rectal tissues through the act of anal intercourse.

The shout of drug-facilitated sexual ecstasy inspired and watched over by the effeminate god of Love was an important religious aspect of Greco-Roman marriage. When early Christians declared their own bridegroom to be the god "Love," they placed their Messiah in a position traditionally filled by Roman gods like Eros and Hymen. And in doing so, they established Jesus as an effeminate facilitator of anal intercourse.

It may seem odd to the modern world that the Romans who lived during the rise of Christianity claimed the followers of Jesus were involved in explicit sexual acts with each other during their "love feasts," but the text of the New Testament itself seems to support this notion. Paul's admonition that a father should marry his daughter if he has any sort of sexual desire for her seems to support pagan suspicions of problems with early Christian sexual morality. It is difficult for the post-classical world to accept the notion that Christians may have actively engaged in sodomy—an act considered taboo by the modern world—but anal intercourse was an important aspect of ancient sexuality.

5:

SACRED SODOMY

*"I concede, my face lacks beauty…
but my enormous cock is gorgeous."*

—PRIAPUS

An erect penis is a work of art, especially if it belongs to a woman. The modern world may openly praise Classical civilization for numerous outstanding contributions to history, but in reality the Greeks and Romans invested much more of their time and treasure in the public celebration of the penis than in any other single social or intellectual pursuit—including the development of democracy—by far. Philosophy, science and free speech certainly sprang from the genius of a few western aristocrats, poets and naturalists, but the phallus permeated every corner of ancient society, from the palaces of the urban affluent to the humble gardens of the rural impoverished.

And, oddly enough, the greatest and most lasting tribute to the power of the erect penis belonged to the primordial she-male gods, the "gynomorphs" who laid the foundation of everything western. It's fair to say that in antiquity erections were impressive, especially on women.

Sacred Erections

Rigid penises permeated the ancient Mediterranean; the Classical phallus made its presence known at religious rites, theatrical performances, social brotherhoods, drinking parties and even civic statuary. Erections appear on statues, in frescoes, on pottery and even in the leather accoutrements worn by actors; the phallus was ubiquitous, and it was seen and felt by all ages and both sexes at any time of the day, in spaces that were both public and private.

Walking the streets in antiquity, young girls were encouraged to suggestively stroke the large erections of the statues of Priapus, as a sort of hopeful nod to future fecundity. Doctors, midwives, priestesses and quacks used dildos made of glass, stone, wood and leather to administer drugs to both men and women via the rectum and the vagina. Priests carried huge erections in processions meant to honor long-established divinities like Dionysus, Demeter and Kore. Gardeners carved and erected wooden statues of Priapus and used the god's notoriously bulbous penis as a weapon against invaders.

The phallus was ubiquitous, and it was seen and felt by all ages and both sexes at any time of the day.

And erections weren't just things of beauty; they were symbols of divine power and cosmic purpose. Priapus, the son of Aphrodite, sported his oversized erection for a very good reason. His phallus wasn't some form of ego-adornment—it was his personal, divine weapon, a means of divine retribution for those in life who choose to reap ill-gotten gains. Zeus had his lightning, Apollo his bow, Poseidon his trident, Hercules his club, and Priapus his penis.

And Priapus didn't just proudly strut around ancient gardens with his larger-than-life erection as a sort of device of vanity; he protected the fruits of the gardener's labors with the threat of sodomy. After all, sodomy was not just a sexual act in antiquity; it was a symbol of the strictest form of divine justice. These are words from the *Priapeia*, spoken by the god from whose name we derive our medical word "priapism," a persistent, unyielding erection: "As long as you refrain from stealing from my garden, I'll allow you to remain as intact as Vesta. But if you fail to restrain yourself, thief, the weapon under my paunch will so stretch your ass-pussy that you will be able to slip right through it."

Priapus' phallus was his personal, divine weapon.

In other words, the gods of the pre-Christian western world didn't tolerate greed; they punished it with painful humiliation. And Priapus was the god of natural justice. His erect penis was a religious weapon used to teach a lesson to anyone who chose to acquire goods at the expense of others.

Aphrodisiacs and Priapism

The ancient phallus is hard for a reason. Greco-Roman physicians, oracles, priests and witches possessed a

BOTANICAL
MEDICINES

myriad of drugs capable of inducing and reducing erections. These pharmaceuticals were derived from animals, plants and even insects, and they were highly effective. According to Pliny, who cites the well-respected botanist Theophrastus, the Greeks even possessed a drug that could make a man ejaculate as many as seventy times without losing his erection.

According to ancient medical sources like the drug expert Dioscorides, of the first century CE, and the physician Galen, of the second century CE, there were several families of aphrodisiacs. Some made the penis hard or "hot" and others made it soft or "cold." These drugs were compound mixtures of plants and animal toxins. Some of these drugs, like Spanish fly, are still used today for the same purposes.

Designer Sex Drugs

T he most prominent of these designer sex drug compounds were given names with the "STR" consonantal root in Latin and Greek. Some were called "satyrion" or "asteria," and even mythic figures like the satyrs bear the linguistic mark of these popular drugs. In antiquity satyrs ran around with erections, just like those who drank the powerful concoction knows as *satyrion*.

Sex drugs like *satyrion* and *asteria* were applied as "anointing oils" in medico-religious contexts. For example, *asteria* contained blister beetle toxin, cannabis (hash oil), opium, and—among other ingredients—hallucinogens derived from plants like nightshade. These potent drugs were compounded with olive oil as a base, to which volatile oils from roses and other fragrant plants were added. The mixture was then applied to a dildo—that is, the dildo was anointed—and then applied by insertion in the rectum or vagina.

Many of the aphrodisiacs, particularly those used by prostitutes, also contained abortifacients. In this way, the same drug promoted sexual activity and reduced the likelihood of pregnancy. This is important, because the act of sex was used as a means of producing oracular vision in antiquity, and not everyone who wanted a religious experience wanted to get pregnant.

The same drug could promote sexual activity and reduce the likelihood of pregnancy.

One of the most interesting of these sex drugs used to anoint the penis was called *baccharis* and ultimately came to Greece and Rome through Lydia. The drug contains saponins that induce smooth muscle contraction. When applied to the rectum, baccharis likely induces anal sphincter spasming; when applied to the cervix, the effect would undoubtedly be uterine contractions. Curiously, the gospel writers report that Mary Magdalen anointed Jesus with this very same costly drug. And Pope Gregory I, in his *Homily 33*, reported that Mary used this specific drug as a sexual stimulant.

Witches and Erections

If you really wanted a sustained erection in antiquity, you needed to visit a witch. Even doctors relied on witches' profound knowledge of botanical drug lore and their experience with poisons.

Romans of the first and second centuries of the Common Era were all but pathologically obsessed by witches and their power over human sexuality. Two of the witches that most stirred the Roman imagination were Circe and her niece Medea. Both were known for their prowess with drugs—so much, Classical scholars are willing to recognize and discuss. However, these two were also known for their ability to sustain and destroy the power of men to become aroused.

The key to their power to enliven and paralyze the male genitalia was the witches' wand. Modern scholars shy away from discussing the practical uses of the accoutrements of witches, but according to the Roman author Petronius, in his aptly named work *Satyricon*, the witches' wand, or "virga" in Latin, was used by priestesses of Priapus in sexual cult practices.

The image of the powerful woman sodomizing her male devotee with her own rigid penis is one of the foundational icons of western civilization.

Petronius, as a courtier of the emperor Nero, lived a life centered on the satisfaction of his appetites and provides many details about the sexual life of the Roman people.

The *virga* was a vehicle for the application of oil-based aphrodisiacs. The Romans recognized that biologically active substances that would be ineffective when swallowed could be directly absorbed by the rectum and vaginal wall. The oil-based aphrodisiacs were no exception; when men came to witches and priestesses to participate in the veneration of gods like Priapus, they were given drugs rectally via the *virga*. This rod was anointed with the drug and then inserted in the rectum. Petronius gives the impression that these men were given a sedative and then restrained—probably for their own safety— before the priestess witches performed rectal stimulation with their *virga*. It's likely that the introduction of the *virga* into the rectum also promoted sexual excitation by massaging the prostate, much as the introduction of an erect penis into the male anus would.

PASSION SLAVE

Sacred Sodomy

According to Petronius, priestess witches used their wands and their drugs to create something best translated as "sacred sodomy," or *sacra pigiciaca* in Latin. And, of course, the image of the religious female authority sodomizing the male was not random, but right out of Classical religious tradition. For the priestesses of Priapus who brought men to orgasm by means of rectal stimulation were performing the same rites as those of the oldest hermaphroditic deities. That is, Roman priestess witches carried on traditions first handed down centuries before by the devotees of Aphrodite-Urania, Phanes and Hermaphroditus, the great she-male goddesses of the ancient world.

The image of the powerful woman sodomizing her male devotee with her own rigid penis is one of the foundational icons of western civilization. Long before Socrates was ever declared to be the wisest of the democratically inclined Athenians by an oracular priestess, Greek priestess-witches sodomized men in the name of hermaphroditic gods in order to create oracles that consistently thwarted the exercise of tyranny. In other words, she-male sodomy promoted democracy.

6:

MEDICATED DILDOS

"A Bull's raging lust is best extinguished by the magic rites of virgins."

—PETRONIUS

The phallus was a powerful sexual symbol in antiquity, but for the Greeks and Romans an erect penis was never just a penis. Modern Freudian baggage aside, ancient dildos, the practical manifestations of artistic phallic depictions, were not mere sexual objects. Rather, they were complex instruments designed for drug delivery as well as valuable religious accoutrements used in cultic practices throughout the Mediterranean.

Ancient physician-priestesses were branded "witches" by the later Christian world.

It would be safe to say that the dildo is history's most maligned religious object. In fact, without the dildo, there would be no oracles or Sibyls. And without those priestesses, the ancient world would never have invented democracy.

The Classical Dildo

Due to modern monotheistic sexual mores, the idea that dildos are somehow valuable for the survival of humanity is a difficult premise to swallow. However, the dildo revealed its own value in western culture when it ended up at the heart of classical civilization's most important medical symbol. The caduceus, the Greek rod surrounded with snakes, was originally an artistic representation of a device that our texts seem to imply was used to apply drugs to the vagina and rectum.

When ancient oracles performed their religious rituals, they were not just acting as priestesses but also as physicians. Modern scholars are confounded by the fact that a considerable percentage of oracular inquiries—questions posed to prophetic priestesses—involved uncertainties about menstruation and child-birth. But within the context of the actual activities of ancient priestly colleges, this makes perfect sense. Ancient priestesses established and refined the practice of ancient pharmacy in order to regulate menstruation and fight disease. These physician-priestesses called the process of us-ing drugs to manipulate the menstrual flow "draw-ing down the moon" and were branded "witches" by the later Christian world.

CADUCEUS

However, ancient drug-savvy priestesses didn't just concern themselves with reproductive issues; they also manipulated the act of coitus with their drugs and used sexual intercourse as a tool of intimate ecstasy in the context of their religious ceremonies.

Wands in Myth

Many myths concerned with ancient gods and goddesses are wrapped up with the use of wands, rods, and staffs made of various materials, tools that were introduced into the rectum or vagina as dildo-shaped medical applicators. The followers of Bona Dea—an ancient Roman goddess worshipped exclusively by women—Priapus and Bacchus, with their secretive female-oriented sexual rites, openly incorporated dildo-driven sexual imagery into their own myths and rituals.

In one such instance of the use of religious dildos, the followers of Bona Dea were described by one Roman author, Juvenal, as being famously involved in highly sexually charged rites:

> "The mysteries of Bona Dea are famous; a time when devotees stimulate their groins with the stiff flute. Plying horns and wine with a singular purpose, these Priapic maenads roll their stunned heads and groan to the goddess. Such a great desire for sex burns in their minds; their moaning is accompanied by explicit gyrations and produces a flood of undiluted sexual desire that flows down their medicated thighs."

The in-and-out thrusting of dildo-shaped magical weapons was a popular image with both Greek and Roman authors. The "undiluted sexual desire that flows down their medicated thighs" is clearly a reference to a mixture of female ejaculate and oils popularly used to lubricate ancient dildos. These dildos were "anointed" with botanicals that classical physicians claimed could significantly enhance sexual arousal. Ancient doctors referred to these drugs as "hardeners," "softeners," "heat-inducers" and "chill-inducers." These stimulants were used in connection with "bracers" and "relaxants," botanical drugs massaged into the labia that heightened the intensity and pleasure of dildo penetration.

Using dildo-applicators was an important aspect of ancient medicine and religion, because priestesses combined sexual union and its concomitant orgasmic ecstasy with rituals meant to produce oracular vision. The survival of cults like those of Priapus, Aphrodite and Cybele was contingent upon the performance of sexual acts involving drugs and dildos. Ancient dildos and dildo-shaped rods used to apply medicines in such cults show up in famous myths stretching from Homer's *Odyssey* to Virgil's *Aeneid* and beyond.

Hard or Soft

Circe, the famous sorceress-goddess who trapped Odysseus and his men on her island, was known for her extensive drug knowledge and her use of a powerful rod that turned men into animals. Homer said that she was "polypharmakon" or drug-savvy. Greek and Roman physicians used the very same word to indicate physicians who relied heavily on drugs to treat disease. And Circe's modus operandi was as clever as it was pharmacologically deceptive. Drawing Odysseus' men into her palace by means of the captivating allure of her incredible beauty and the overwhelming sex appeal of her female assistants, Circe enticed Odysseus' men and offered them a meal laced with drugs. She then took advantage of them with her magical rod.

Consuming the meal with its concealed drugs, Odysseus' men suddenly became susceptible to Circe's overwhelming magic. The witch rigorously applied her rod and turned them all into pigs. Homer actually uses the imagery of Circe "striking" the men with the rod, the very same image used of the application of the ancient "virga," the rectal medicated rod used by priestesses of Priapus by means of a back and forth thrusting action.

The in-and-out thrusting of these dildo-shaped magical weapons was a popular image with both Greek and Roman authors. In his *Satyricon*, Petronius, a Roman

HERMES

The secret in the encounter of Odysseus and Circe is the use of drugs by both parties to induce uncontrollable sexual appetites.

author of the first century CE, mimicked the episode of Circe's application of pig-transforming drugs in his clever fictional account of an Odysseus-like character who ended up on the business end of a priestess's medicated dildo: "She took out a leather dildo, coated it with a thin layer of oil mixed with pepper and bruised nettle seed, and gradually inserted it in my rectum."

An Impotence Cure

In Petronius' story, the medicated dildo used by the priestess of Priapus is used in the very same manner as that of Circe and Odysseus. Petronius' narrative features a sexual paramour and devotee of Priapus named Circe, who involves the main character in the use of drugs as sexual stimulants to cure his sexual impotence. Ultimately, the witch-priestess only indirectly succeeds, and the god Hermes is given the credit for restoring the erection rather than Circe and her companions.

Petronius' story makes good sense as a parody of Homer's *Odyssey*. In the *Odyssey* it is Hermes who supplies a potent antidote-like drug to Odysseus that ultimately enables the hero to defeat Circe—and when Homer mentions defeat, he really means sexual conquest, for the two characters end up locked in sexual intercourse at the climax of their battle.

The secret in the encounter of Odysseus and Circe is the use of drugs by both parties to induce uncontrollable sexual appetites. Circe gives Odysseus' men a drug that makes them amenable to penetration with her rod. And this rod then turns them into animals. In the same way, Petronius' main character is drugged against his will, bound and penetrated in a sexual rite meant to facilitate the worship of Priapus, the god of the erection. In Homer, Odysseus is able to fight to maintain control—much to the surprise of Circe—with additional drugs. And Circe, as a result, insists that he copulate with her directly. Both stories hinge on the effective use of drugs as sexual stimulants and the use of wands or dildos for the application of sex drugs.

Myths of the Bona Dea employ the use of the "virga" to incite the sexual desire of the female as well—in this case the goddess herself is urged to sexual excitement with the virga. And this virga is the same wand as the famous caduceus, the long-established symbol of Hermes. When used by Hermes, the snake-covered rod is known to induce exhaustion and sleep, very much like the rods used by Circe and the devotees of Priapus. Apparently the sacred post-coital sleep that followed hard upon the use of ancient medicated dildos was a sacramental method of inducing oracular vision in ancient cults.

Rectal and vaginal routes for the administration of ancient drugs were just more-effective means of consuming medicines.

Opening the Gateway

Ancient priestesses had specific reasons for using dildos in their religious practices. The most basic was the application of drugs meant to affect physiology. Ancient physicians employed a limited number of techniques for applying drugs. Medicines could be swallowed, snorted, applied to the skin, and even inhaled when burned. Each method of application had its own drawbacks and benefits. Some drugs, like wormwood, were so unpalatable that oral administration was difficult, particularly with younger patients. Greek and Roman physicians also acknowledged that different drugs worked well when applied to the skin or a membrane, but not so well when swallowed.

Rectal and vaginal routes for the administration of ancient drugs were just more-effective means of consuming medicines. The colon, in particular, is well suited to the absorption of fluids, and enemas have been used as medicines in many different cultures across the globe. In addition, rectal and vaginal tissues allow for the circumvention of the harsh environment of the stomach, where strong acids tend to break up botanical chemicals that act as medicines in the bloodstream.

The classical world used rectally administered drugs for medical reasons, but ancient priestesses also applied drugs in this manner to induce oracular visions. One of the most famous and underemphasized scenes involving the use of drugs for oracular effect is found in the story of Aeneas's descent into the underworld.

In the sixth book of the *Aeneid*, Virgil tells us that Aeneas sought out a priestess of Hecate to accompany him to the underworld. Virgil is very clear that his record of Aeneas' trip to

The sibyl emphasizes that it is Aeneas' sexual desire that makes his quest possible.

Hades with this sibyl reveals elements of an oracular cult deemed to be sacred, and he asks the gods to guide his poetry with respect for the esoteric ritual he exposes—an ancient way of hedging any ill-will the gods might have borne toward him for publicly revealing details of mystery cult performances.

Use of the Ramus

Virgil tells his audience that the priestess employs a "ramus" in order to transport Aeneas to the underworld. The Latin word "ramus" signified a branch of a tree or a penis-like object. The sibyl tells Aeneas to find this ramus and bring it to her for their transit to Hades:

> "A shady tree conceals a secret rod sacred to the Queen of the Underworld. This y-shaped branch, gilded with gold both on its projections and on its highly flexible base...serves as a holy instrument in the worship of the beautiful infernal bride."

Virgil's sibyl reports that this wooden rod is highly flexible and gilded with gold. After Aeneas finds the rod, he brings it to the sibyl, who orders everyone else to leave and then leads the hero into a cave. Once inside

the cave Aeneas is enabled to cross the threshold of the
earth-realm into the underworld by means of the vibrat-
ing ramus, or the gilded rod.

The Latin used by Virgil to describe the scene is unmistakably sexually charged. Even the sibyl emphasizes
this by directly asserting that it is Aeneas' sexual desire
(*amor*) that makes the quest possible. And the last time
Virgil wrote about a cave in the Aeneid was when Aeneas and Dido consummated their symbolic marriage in
a dark cave during a storm.

The Sibyl used the ramus, or rod, to open a portal
whereby the two could then enter the oracular dream
world of Hades in order to satisfy Aeneas' desire to see
his dead father. The portal is described at the end of the
book as having two openings, and is directly associated
with dreaming.

The Pythagorean Connection

T he followers of Pythagoras taught that the ramus, as
a symbol of the Greek letter upsilon, was a branched
rod with three terminations in the shape of the English "Y." As a magico-medical device, it is likely that
the ramus was coated with gold to facilitate its use as a
medicated dildo. Gold is hypoallergenic and thus recognized in antiquity as a body-friendly metal. In addition,
the soft gold coat of the ramus would have ensured its
usefulness as a flexible rectal or vaginal applicator.

The Sibyl's guided tour to the underworld, as part of
a "mystery" performance, was coupled with the image
of the young priestess bride joining herself to the older

male groom. The two sexes became one by facilitating the penetration of three portals. Opening these portals allowed Aeneas and the sibyl to come to the climax of their journey in a moment of blissful serenity that preceded a profound sleep.

By means of the medicated, dildo-shaped ramus, the young priestess was able to fulfill the desire of Aeneas to travel to otherworldly locations. The same act is replicated in Petronius' *Satyricon*, where the main character is sexually penetrated by a medicated dildo applied by drug-wielding priestesses of the underworld gods. These same priestesses were responsible for the oracular pronouncements of the ancient world that consistently propelled the classical world toward democratic governance. It is fair to say that medicated dildos were active components of ancient religions that provided the foundations for modern medicine, science and democracy.

7:

ANAL PORTAL

"We mortals are children of erotic desire."

—ARISTOPHANES

O racular priestesses applied dildos to the rectum in order to transport devotees of the infernal gods to the distant dreamscape of the underworld. Medicated anal probes, made of gilded wood, leather and stone, covered with potent drug mixtures, were vehicles of visionary transport. The Greco-Roman world used numerous botanicals and animal-derived toxins to compound mixtures of sexual stimulants that were applied to the rectum and vagina. These designer sex drugs, when applied by means of sexual stimulation by young female priestesses, enabled oracle-seekers to visualize spectacular new worlds.

Visiting the Underworld

T he most frequented site of dildo-induced transport was the underworld, or Erebus as it was known to the ancients. Priestesses known as necromancers, including oracles and witches, practiced their medical arts at places deemed by classical civilization to be "portals" to Erebus. The women who initiated these practices were not mature women at all, but young girls.

The Greeks called the priestesses who initiated this form of dreamy, drug-induced transport to the underworld "korai." The singular form of this word, "kore," denotes a period of life rather than a specific age. The kore was the time in a young woman's life when she was first sexually developed, and it represented the natural flowering or bloom of femininity. A girl was considered a kore until her first pregnancy, at which time she entered into the next phase of feminine existence.

Until late Roman antiquity, oracular priestesses were exclusively korai. Their knowledge of drugs was extensive and their training was supervised by older women known as "root-cutters." These women were drug collectors whose age made them incapable of serving as oracles, but their pharmaceutical and medical training was invaluable to the activities of oracular shrines which they served. Aged priestesses taught young korai how to perform necromantic cultic rituals.

Necromantic rituals are embedded in much of the myth surrounding divinities and heroes. Not all gods were worshiped by necromancers, but the gods who were objects of necromantic veneration were wildly popular throughout the Mediterranean. The principal necromantic deities were Cybele, Persephone, Hecate and Dionysus. Each god was involved with specific gender transformations, particularly the unification of both sexes into one pluri-potential she-male known to the Greeks as the "aiolomorph." Aiolomorphs were a specific group of bi-gendered gynomorphs whose provenance was rituals associated with the underworld.

The term "aiolomorph" was derived from the color-changing sheen given off by the scales of certain snakes, which appeared to change their appearance as they reflected light in different patterns. The pre-classical Greek world considered this alteration of colors to be a sort of transformation. Aiolomorphic gods were divinities capable of transforming themselves.

Priestesses understood that the penetrative sexual stimulation of men accompanied by drug use was a reliable means of initiating visions.

Dildos For Men

Aiolomorphs were typically serpent-associated divinities, whose gender-bending abilities were at the heart of their cult worship; aiolomorphic gods were characterized by the ability to transform from one sexual state to another. For example, Cybele was able to morph from male to female; Persephone embodied the sexual transformation of puberty; Hecate was a cyclical triform aiolomorph, capable of manifesting masculine, feminine and bi-gendered gynomorphic traits.

Priestesses who venerated aiolomorphic gods in Greco-Roman literature understood one important fact: the penetrative sexual stimulation of men accompanied by drug use was a reliable means of initiating vivid dreams or "visions." While dildos were frequently used for the sexual gratification of women and the application of gynecological medicines, Greek and Roman oracles and sibyls understood that the rectal stimulation of men coupled with the application of drugs absorbed by the colon was a potent means of initiating male novices into the mystery rites of necromancy.

The proper application of a penis-shaped object or anal probe to the male rectum, and the concomitant stimulation of the prostate and associated reproductive tissues, is certainly conducive to sexual arousal. Collecting semen from bulls for the sake of artificial insemination today is performed in exactly the same manner. Technicians trained in collection of semen insert metallic probes into the bull's anus in order to stimulate erection and forced ejaculation without direct penile stimulation.

Forcing bulls to orgasm and ejaculate is no different than forcing men to do the same. The physiological response to forced rectal stimulation is the same in both mammals. The inhabitants of the ancient Mediterranean clearly understood that anal stimulation of human males could produce an ejaculatory response, and this act was incorporated into the mystery rituals of oracular cults concerned with gender transformation and necromancy.

MAN-BULL
INSEMINATOR

Dionysus Visits Erebus

One of the most striking examples of the connections among religion, necromancy and anal-probe stimulation is found in the worship of Dionysus. One of Dionysus' great accomplishments was his visit to Erebus, where he resurrected his own mother and brought her to Olympus to live with the gods. The myth of the god's visit to the underworld was so wildly popular that it became the subject of a comic play of Aristophanes. And the myth famously culminated in rigorous anal stimulation with a dildo.

Dionysus, like Odysseus and Aeneas, was able to accomplish his journey to the underworld by following the cult practices of the necromancers. One of these necromancers showed Dionysus the "portal" to Erebus, and when the god returned to the Earth from the depths, he fulfilled a necromantic ritual in honor of the man who showed him the art of journeying to the underworld. In this instance, the necromancer became the "lover" of the person making the journey, and their

Dionysus was able to accomplish his journey to the underworld by following the cult practices of the necromancers.

sexual relationship called for the necromancer to anally penetrate the initiate.

Unfortunately, the necromancer died before Dionysus could return, but the god fulfilled the cult practice by sitting upon a dildo placed at the gravesite of the deceased. Clement of Alexandria, an early Christian Church father, was openly critical of the myth and its embedded necromantic cult practices, writing in *Exhortation to Greeks*, "Honoring this obligation to his lover, Dionysus rushes to his grave and commits lewd acts. After cutting off a branch from a fig tree, he whittles it into the shape of the male genitalia, and then sits on it, fulfilling his promise to the dead. In memory of this mystery experience, Phalloi have been erected in different cities to Dionysus."

Phallic Pillars

C lement tells us the god's act of anal self-penetration was memorialized by the erection of large phallic pillars across Greece and Italy. Archaeologists frequently label phallic pillars like these as artifacts of "fertility cults," but fertility had nothing at all to do with Dionysus bringing himself to the point of ejaculation by means of the anal insertion of a medicated dildo. The god was not trying to impregnate anything or anyone; he was inducing sexual ecstasy by means of anal stimulation.

The creation of a dildo from a broken tree branch falls right in line with the Roman tradition of the use of a "ramus" as a rod-like device used to transport men to the dream-world of Erebus. The myth of Dionysus' visit to the underworld carefully preserves actual necromantic rituals.

Necromantic priestesses and witches used this forced, drug-facilitated, anal stimulation of men to create dream-like hallucinatory states in which they believed the living could commune with the dead. Most of these ancient oracles were young, post-pubertal priestesses, but sometimes they were young, castrated, post-pubertal males. And much to the chagrin of the early Church, Dionysus and his followers employed post-pubertal boys to apply the anal probe, whereas Jesus and the early Christian priesthood insisted on the use of pre-pubertal children for resurrection rites that resembled necromantic initiation.

Jesus' Sex Drug

And what was the reason for putting a dildo up a man's rectum in order to facilitate visions of a necromantic journey to the underworld? The answer for both the pagan world and the followers of Jesus was exactly the same: resurrection.

In the Gospel of Mark, it was reported that Mary presented Jesus with compounded substances contained in an "alabastron," a penis-shaped container used to store designer sex drugs in antiquity. Shortly thereafter, Jesus went to the Garden of Gethsemane with three of his disciples and a naked boy, where Mark 14 tells us he was arrested by local authorities.

Any ancient Roman would clearly identify Jesus' actions as necromantic.

When Jesus took his sex-drug containing, penis-shaped "alabastron" from the prostitute Mary, and entered a period of great temptation in a public park during late-

night hours, in the com-
pany of a naked child,
he was acting in a way
that any ancient Roman
would clearly identify as
"necromantic."

Phanes was a masculine god with a penis, but he was also perfectly feminine and had both a vagina and breasts.

The purpose of anal penetration, in a dark or night-time setting, by pagan necromancers, was the induction of the oracular dream state and the concomitant initiation of an inductee into the reality of the existence of Erebus. The witches who followed Hecate and Priapus were famous for initiating these very same rites. They opened portals to the underworld by using sexual devices and medicines to facilitate visions. After Christian bishops gained political authority in late antiquity, these women were actively persecuted for their religious practices and deemed to be children of the Devil.

Forbidden Resurrection

But why were these women so vigorously prosecuted? Because witches and oracles performed necromantic rituals in order to raise the dead and to send the living to the underworld and back. And resurrection was strictly forbidden for anyone but the Christian Messiah. In the Christian mind, only God himself should have the power to resurrect the dead.

For centuries witches actively pursued raising a powerful dual-gendered god from the underworld; this resurrected god was a divinity older than all the Olympians. He was celebrated under many different names.

The followers of Dionysus and Demeter called him Iacchos, the celebrants of Isis called him Osiris, and the Orphics called him Phanes: "I call upon dual gendered Protogonos, the great navigator of the ether...source of the blessed immortals and men, seed of creation venerated in many secret rites...I invoke you by the name Phanes, Lord Priapus."

Phanes, the invisible god manifested by the followers of necromancy, was the earliest dual-gendered creator of the Greco-Roman world. He was a masculine god with a penis, but he was also perfectly feminine and had both a vagina and breasts.

Zeus, the leader of Greek, Roman and even Etruscan pantheons, recognized the value of the dual-gendered god, and "swallowed" him within his own body in order to absorb his strengths. The followers of Orpheus, who were active as early as the sixth century BCE, taught that Zeus was himself involved in gender transformations. In their eyes, the god Phanes was the embodiment of the erect, medicated phallus. They believed Zeus recognized that performing self-penetration in the same manner as Dionysus was the ultimate means of receiving the god into his body. According to the Orphics, Zeus "swallowed" Phanes and was thus transformed (or gender-bent) into the she-male warrior goddess called Athena.

Phanes was symbolized as a cloud of light, a god with both genders whose physical form was entirely invisible. Phanes was given the title "Protogonos," which can be translated both as "First-Produced" and "Primeval-Gender."

The Gospel of Judas

Jesus and his apostles seized upon mystery initiations of their time that employed the image of Phanes and his value as a divine catalyst of sexually transformative initiation. In the gospel of Judas, translated from its Coptic original, history has preserved the teachings of Jesus ostensibly handed down by his disciple Judas. Unsurprisingly, Jesus says things that are lifted right out of ancient necromantic mystery initiations involving Phanes and his use of medicated dildos.

The Coptic traditions that preserve these necromantic teachings of Jesus originate in northern Egypt, where early Church fathers founded catechetical schools. These catechetical schools trained young initiates in the "mysteries" of the Church using exorcists trained to purge young boys of their sexual desire for women. This ritual rape of pre-pubescent boys was designed to purge them of the control of Eve, the female divine

JUDAS AND JESUS

force that corrupts all of mankind. The same region of Egypt was associated with the activities of Mark, the gospel writer who claimed that Jesus was arrested after receiving a medicated dildo from Mary. Mark also related that Jesus was arrested while in the presence of a naked boy.

The gospel of Judas betrays the reliance of the early Christians of Egypt on sexually explicit, necromantic traditions attributed to their Messiah: "Jesus said, 'Come, that I may teach you about secrets no person has ever seen. For there exists a great and boundless realm, whose extent no generation of angels has seen, in which there is a great invisible spirit'...And a luminous cloud appeared there. He said, 'Let an angel come into being as my attendant.' A great angel, the enlightened divine Self-Generated, emerged from the cloud."

The gospel of Judas uses the very same terminology employed by necromantic cults of Greece and Rome. The religious epithets are the same; the rituals are the same; and the desired outcomes are the same. In the mind of ancient pagans and Christians, resurrection of the dead was a reality of life. Jesus and the followers of Dionysus shared a desire to bring the "First-Begotten" out of the grave. And the only way to do so was to open a portal to the underworld by means of a long-established ritual of masculine anal penetration using a medicated dildo and a young sacrificial medium.

8:

AROUSING THE DEAD

"Grant my drugs the power of arousal, witch goddess, and with my concoctions preserve the germinal semen of life, established in the flames of desire."

—SENECA

There is a good reason ancient witches became experts in the use of sexual drugs: they understood that the manipulation of sexuality was a means of transport from the mundane to the magical. Ancient philosophers studied logic, mathematics and natural science in pursuit of personal enlightenment. Clerics read "signs" of the sky and prognosticated on their oracular significance in order to avert disaster and honor the gods.

Statesmen pursued oratory and law in order to perpetuate the machinery of ancient governance. And—as equally valued members of ancient society—Greco-Roman witches studied the ecstasy of sexuality in order to resurrect a bi-gendered creator, a gynomorphic god who was the key to unlocking a multi-dimensional universe.

Witches

For the young priestesses who served gods such as Hecate, Priapus, and Dionysus, the secrets of the

Ancient witches were part of a long religious and medical tradition that predates written history. natural world were not just for the theoretical musings of natural scientists. These educated women took an active approach to the cosmos by advancing the notion that the world around them, particularly the human body, could be actively manipulated; they believed they were not just spectators of the cosmic dream, but active participants in the progress of the universe's drama.

Ancient witches were part of a long religious and medical tradition that predates written history. They were a bridge between the shaman of early human civilization and the philosopher of the classical era. The earliest written records of Greek, Roman and Etruscan civilization are replete with drugs and drug recipes used by priestesses and witches. The witch's understanding of drugs predates the written word. Even the palace records of the Minoans and Mycenaeans, the earliest ancestors of the Greeks to leave written documents, show an awareness of the use of botanicals as drugs.

Witches were never passive. They actively engaged their discipline and subject matter in order to advance their cause. With a clear, unified agenda, and laborious training in their arts, ancient witches claimed to be able to harness the power of the natural world to perform supernatural feats. Their miracles were based in the reality of sexuality, as the witch Canidia said in Horace's *Epodes*: "With my own voice I am able to draw down the moon; I can arouse the dead once cremated; I can concoct drugs of sexual desire."

Witches accomplished the impossible by manipulating the mundane. They scoured their environments for the tools necessary to alter the natural world; and they used the act of human sexual intercourse as a springboard to affect their supernatural tinkering. It's fair to say that the heart of ancient witchcraft was sexuality. There is a good reason that so many ancient spells are concerned with intercourse: witches believed sex was the cosmic magic that gave them their power.

Drugs

The desire to bend nature led priestesses of Hecate, Priapus and Dionysus to the use of potent plant and animal substances; these chemicals had dramatic effects on human physiology. Powdered aconite was lethal in very small doses; opium latex from the poppy, mixed with the juices of the deadly nightshade plant, caused benumbed ecstasy; ground blister beetles made for an hours-long, irreducible erection in men.

One of the drugs used in antiquity that has entirely escaped the radar of modern scholars is snake venom. Venoms of various snake species were used as

REPTILIAN DRUGS

medicines, regulators of menstruation and weaponized poisons. The Greeks and Romans recognized that snake venoms were potent biologically active substances. These venoms, when applied to the human body, caused physiological changes that were readily observable by natural scientists and laymen alike, and were frequently quite dramatic.

An elaborate mythology of snake-lore appears in the earliest recorded Greek texts. Snakes are presented as gods, guardians and demons. For example, the followers of Bacchus wrapped snakes around their heads. The Furies, punishers of cold-blooded murder, lashed their victims with living snakes. And witches, such as Horace's Canidia, were characterized as avid proponents of snake-derived drugs: "What sort of drug is this that rages in my chest? Has someone secretly mixed viper venom into the botanicals I have been given? Has Canidia prepared a meal meant to prepare a sacrifice?"

In the *Epodes* by the celebrated Roman poet Horace, Canidia is presented as a cunning witch involved in the preparation of an infernal sacrifice—that is, a ritual sacrifice to the gods of the underworld. As a witch or sorceress, Canidia uses snake venom, specifically viper venom, to prepare sacrifices for slaughter.

Vipers produce venom that affects the ability of blood to coagulate. As predators, these snakes use hemorrhagic venoms to kill prey, but the complex protein toxins they employ may also help prepare their food sources for digestion. Venom glands in reptiles are just evolutionarily developed saliva glands, and the poisons they synthesize are physiologically active when injected directly into the bloodstream.

Several popular mystery religions of Greece and Rome relied heavily on the use of vipers during their celebrations, and the iconography of this particular reptile regu-larly intrudes into the literature and artistic representa-tions of these same cults. Within the practices of these cults, vipers typically appear in the context of oracular transformation. That is, the vipers are represented as agents of maniacal metamorphosis; they enable mystery initiates to assume the madness characteristic of gyno-morphic gods like Dionysus.

Other snake species also creep into mythological references in very specific ways that reflect the ancient world's fascination with gender-switching and sexual manipulation. For example, the great python of Delphi, the snake that originally guarded the famous oracle, is fluidly described as both male and female by ancient poets. The Greeks didn't differentiate between two Delphic pythons of different gender but made it ap-pear that the one serpent-guardian of the oracle could appear as either sex. The Orphics called this snake-god Korybas and gave him/her the title "aiolomorph," the Greek epithet reserved for gender-switching divinities.

Stars

Priestesses and sorceresses who pioneered the use of snake venoms for the regulation of menstruation be-

MOONLIGHT MAGIC

lieved in a universe composed of various overlapping planes. The ancient witch's cosmos is strikingly similar to the multiverse of modern cosmologists who study astrophysics. Witches like Medea, Circe and Canidia believed that the universe was divided into three "realms." These dimension-like realms were given the names Earth, Olympus and Erebus.

According to Greek accounts of the origins of the universe, the three realms of existence all possess basic elements and unique inhabitants. Earth was believed to be the realm of "air," the element consumed by mortals. Olympus was a plane inhabited by gods who breathe ether. And Erebus was a realm of demonic powers who breathe and ingest "dark matter."

The Greco-Roman realms of existence are very much like overlapping dimensions of reality. The inhabitants of each realm are invisible to the other realms but can communicate and interact under specific, controlled circumstances. Witches were most interested in the interactions of Erebus—the underworld—with the world of earthly mortals.

Ancient mythographers recorded traditions that the gods of Erebus could only visit Earth by accessing "portals" or gateways through collapsed stars. Due to the fact that these immortal beings and infernal demons breathed darkness or dark matter, it was necessary to remove or destroy light sources in order to sustain their travel. Poets like Claudian, of the late 4th century CE, taught that the dark matter of Erebus neither reflected nor absorbed light, and thus was incompatible with the Earth realm, where light is abundant. When the gods of Erebus visited Earth, they were forced to remain within dark-matter bubbles in order to sustain themselves as creatures of darkness.

Underworld Gateways

The power to "draw down the stars" in order to open gateways to the underworld became the purview of witches. By employing poisons that contained the power to manipulate the basic elements of the cosmos, these witches believed they were able to enable the gods of the under-world to access the Earth realm. The element-manipulating powers of their drugs manifested themselves by alterations in sexuality—which witches viewed as alterations of the generative power of their bi-gendered goddesses. Their drugs could sexually enflame their victims or stifle their arousal with the force of cold chill, as in Seneca's *Medea*:

Witches believed the gods of the underworld were readily available for consultation and interference in the activities of the Fates, the goddesses who guides human affairs.

> *"After she (Medea) called out every sort of poi-sonous snake, she gathered together her accursed herbs…She picked the death-dealing plants and milked the snakes of their venom and mixed them… the wild force of fire was in some, the power of numbing frost in others."*

The purpose of using these drugs was the attraction or liberation of underworld deities and/or demons. That is, these witches believed the gods of the underworld were readily available for consultation and interference in the activities of the Fates—the goddesses who guided human affairs. Bringing them up from the underworld was a prerequisite for forecasting the future.

Summoning the bi-gendered queen-goddess of the witches was a necessary step in commanding the forces of the underworld—the realm where all mortals eventually end up. This powerful goddess, Hecate, and her masculine manifestations, were all guardians of the gateways to Erebus. Witches summoned Hecate with sacrifice in order to access her power to open portals to the underworld.

Ancient priestesses and sorceresses viewed the underworld as a realm or dimension of the universe accessible through cosmic portals. Using their pharmacological craft, they claimed the ability to open these portals for would-be travelers and for those brave enough to consult the dead. The Oracles of the Dead were valuable oracular cults that influenced the science and politics of the pre-Christian west. It was the aim of these cults to summon a prominent bi-gendered goddess who could assist in the manipulation of the physical world.

It's not at all difficult to see why the bishops of the early Christian church moved the Roman emperor to declare the activity of "witches" to be illegal and prosecutable by execution. The sexual magic of Greco-Roman witches presented an impediment to the spread of Christian mystery rites that openly condemned communication with any of the underworld divinities. Church fathers condemned the use of pagan magic, but they could not entirely wipe out the influence of witches on the Roman population. Drugs used by witches to treat gynecological problems had become an important aspect of ancient medicine. Killing off individual witches did not put an end to their broad influence and practices. Sexuality and magic were intimately tied together through the use of pharmaceuticals by doctors and midwives; Christianity tried in vain to wipe out the influence of ancient witches.

9:

THE FIRST GENDER

"The mortal nourished the snake's offspring,
which licked his ears and gave him the
maddening gift of vision."

—HESIOD

Greco-Roman witchcraft was nothing like the medieval images we moderns perpetuate of warty old crones laboring over their cauldrons while casting spells and turning little boys into toads. On the contrary, the most powerful classical sorceresses found in myth were goddesses; and these goddess-witches of antiquity were young, beautiful girls who were predominantly interested in capturing the affections of their paramours, not in soothing the rigors of the aging process with incantations and nature worship. Contrary to modern feminist ideology, classical civilization believed age was a curse of mortals, and as a result ancient gods were portrayed as existing perpetually in the bloom of youth. Sorceresses were no exception.

The Fallacy

Modern pagans, goddess worshippers, and wiccans spend millions of dollars annually on books, tarot cards, clothing, herbal products, and self-help advice.

Authors, motivational speakers and self-proclaimed priestesses peddle their wares in a booming industry that is founded upon a single historical fallacy. That fallacy is grounded in the 20th century's creation of a triform

There is no ancient Maiden–Mother–Crone goddess in classical myth.

witch-goddess made up of Maiden-Mother-Crone components. Unfortunately, there is no ancient Maiden-Mother-Crone goddess in classical myth. The model is strictly a modern invention.

Perpetuated by presses like Llewellyn, publisher of *Maiden, Mother, Crone: The Myth & Reality of the Triple Goddess* by D. J. Conway, and by authors with no training in Greek, Latin or ancient literature, the Maiden-Mother-Crone model of the ancient goddess has captured the self-helping imagination of the modern world. But it lacks genuine historical authority. And it mars the genuine recognition and celebration of the accomplishments of classical women who were imprisoned and executed for their activities as "witches." It's ironic, but revisionist history is its own worst enemy.

As a result of the skewed view of women's history presented by feminist scholars trying to fit the square peg of the classical world into a post-modern round hole, the genuine contribution of women to western civilization has been predominantly hidden from view. Women following Greco-Roman temple traditions created the first forms of western medicine and pharmacy, and even pioneered the scientific theory. Perhaps most impor-

The earliest Greek oracles and sorceress-sibyls were all teenagers. tantly, oracular priestesses and their sorceress counterparts propelled the Greeks toward the formation of a democratic form of governance and even prevented the Romans from embracing absolute tyranny during the Roman Republic.

The Maiden-Mother-Crone goddess exists nowhere in classical literature, but her fabrication has a very practical purpose. The model is an excellent cultural salve for the realities of the aging process; it instills in its adherents feelings of self-value in the face of an ever-approaching mortality. But it also obscures the real triform goddess figure and its historical adherents, who assisted the ancient world in developing concepts as valuable as science, philosophy and democracy.

She Has a Penis

The problem with the modern model of the triform goddess is that feminists of the 20th century intentionally castrated her. In the eyes of the ancient world, the all-powerful creator goddess was perfectly feminine, but she was also young and sported a proud-if-not-angry penis. The proof is preserved in the amber of the Greek language itself. Greek epithets indicating the "triform" nature of the goddess refer to her manifestation as male, female and bi-gendered—not young, motherly and old.

The triform Hecate had nothing to do with a woman's transition from youth to mid-life and old age. The earliest Greek oracles and sorceress-sibyls were all teenagers; the older generation of witches vacated these positions on reaching middle age because they believed that losing youth's bloom was proof that they had also lost the gifts that made them close to the gods.

Hecate was referred to as a triform in the same manner as numerous other gods. Like other Olympians and Chthonian deities, Hecate was depicted as pos-sessing three dominant "types," and these forms were characterized by attributes that were masculine, femi-nine and bi-gendered. As Selene, goddess of the moon, the triform goddess was the feminine oracular voice of the cyclical cosmos. As Artemis, she was the masculine hunter and slayer who tracked down her prey and killed them with poison arrows. As Hecate she was the youth-ful, bi-gendered gate-keeper who shepherded the shades of the underworld, much like Chthonian Hermes. Hecate was not unusual; each Greek god was part of a unique triform divinity.

Hecate's triform unity was essential and significant to her Mediterranean aco-lytes. Ancient witches per-formed night-time sacrifices in order to summon their bi-gendered deity. And surprisingly, they attempted to resurrect this gynomorph for a very practical reason: bringing the gynomorphic creator goddess into the world was an attempt to establish the predominance of justice in human affairs.

TRIFORM
GODDESS

Return of Justice

Resurrecting the bi-gendered creator was a prelude to the return of Dike, the Greek goddess Justice, who was the last of the Olympians to abandon the greedy generation of mortals who currently inhabit the Earth. As the great creator or "first element," this goddess—with a penis—was responsible for the entire cosmos, as is clear from the *Argonautica Orphica:* "Firstly, ancient Khaos's stern Ananke (Inevitability), and Khronos (Time), who bred within his boundless coils Aither (Light) and two-sexed, two-faced, glorious Eros [Phanes], ever-born Nyx's (Night's) father, whom latter men call Phanes, for he first was manifested."

The Greeks portrayed this bi-gendered creator goddess as a perfect mixture of masculinity and femininity. She was called by various names like Phanes and Eros, depending on the context of the element in which she ruled. When she came from the ether she was Phanes, from the air she was Eros, and from the dark matter she was Hecate.

Each manifestation of the bi-gendered creator brought specific cultural connotations or baggage that was readily recognized by the ancient world. For example, Hecate was a representative of Erebus and therefore one of the guardians of familial justice—the retribution of murdered souls. Eros, on the other hand, as an ethereal being of Olympus, was an agent of Aphrodite-Ura-

Each Greco-Roman triform goddess had a basic hermaphroditic form that represented the primal element of the universe.

nia, and therefore enforced the justice or "nemesis" that accompanied the powers of cosmic attraction. Phanes, the invisible, god of the air, was associated with the generation of animal life and the attraction of one atom or element for another.

The Elemental Source

T he bi-gendered gynomorph, who was one of the three members of the triform goddesses, represented the earliest cosmic manifestation of divinity. That is, each Greco-Roman triform goddess had a basic hermaphroditic form that represented the primal element of the universe. This elemental, bi-gendered form of the goddess could take various forms, like those of Hecate, Phanes or even Venus, as John Lydus of the 6th century

CE explained in *De Mensibus*: "Venus is the nature of all perceptible things, that is, the first potential, whom the oracles call Asteria and Urania..."

The bi-gendered Venus was known to the Greeks as Aphrodite-Urania, and as John Lydus tells us, was both masculine and feminine in form. This manifestation

YOUTHFUL ARTEMIS

of Venus was the creator who gave life to all aspects of the natural world. In addition, she also gave life to living creatures. But most importantly, Venus and other bi-gendered entities created the division of life that resulted in the sexes. That is, the gynomorphs created gender.

The Orphic theogonies, a set of Greek cosmogonies—accounts of the origins of the gods and the universe—illustrate how the bi-gendered goddess created two genders from a single source. There is this, for example, from a source known as *Theogonies Fragment 54*:

> "Khronos (Time), the serpent, has offspring, three in number: moist Aither (Light), unbounded Khaos (Air), and as a third, misty Erebos (Darkness) .
> . . Among these, he says, Khronos (Time) generated an egg—this tradition too making it generated by Khronos, and born 'among' these because it is from these that the third Intelligible triad is produced [Protogonos-Phanes]. What is this triad, then? The egg; the dyad of the two natures inside it (male and female) [Ouranos, Heaven, and Gaia, Earth], and the plurality of the various seeds between [Phanes, Life]."

In this myth, Khronos, a hermaphroditic god, gave birth to an egg containing both sexes. The combination of the two sexes into one was called Phanes, the bi-gendered first element. And of course, Phanes brought about the splitting of himself, as an egg, into two distinct genders, male and female. This splitting is typically carried out by either a serpent or a reaping instrument. In other words, the masculine penis is cut away from the feminine and the two sexes are born. This Greek explanation of the origin of the sexes is the exact opposite of the Judeo-Christian myth, which asserts that the male was created first and the female from him.

The Greek explanation of the origin of the sexes is that the masculine penis is cut away from the feminine and the two sexes are born, the exact opposite of the Judeo-Christian myth.

It's important to realize that the ancient world used this paradigm to explain the variation of the sexes. However, it is even more critical to understand that the Greeks and Romans viewed the sexes as alternating versions of a single hermaphroditic entity that preceded all of creation. In other words, hermaphrodites were the oldest and most natural gender, while males and females were their descendants.

When the Greco-Roman world worshipped gods like Hecate, Venus and Phanes, it did so out of respect for the primal role of hermaphrodites in the creation of life. Ancient witches did not venerate the chronological phases of female life. Sorceresses were not interested in feeling good about their impending old age and death; they were motivated by a desire to celebrate the cosmic mystery of the triform nature of life: the magical transition from the form of a hermaphrodite to the form of a female and finally to the form of a male.

10:

ETRUSCAN MIRRORS

"I declare that one day a woman will bear a hermaphrodite having all the male parts and all the parts that female women manifest."

—SIBYLLINE ORACLE

Nature provided the model for the gods. The Greeks, Romans and Etruscans based their understanding of the immortal gods on the natural forces that rule the universe. The bi-gendered gods of these cultures were the logical precursors of sexed creatures. Just as all elements of the cosmos derive from a single mixed, primordial element, so the two genders must come from a single sex that contained both the masculine and the feminine. Thus, the re-combination of the two genders into a hermaphroditic unity was nature's way of restoring its most basic elements into a unified principle.

The concept of restoring the bi-gendered hermaphrodite went hand-in-hand in the ancient world with the Etruscan fascination with mirrors. Of all the archaeological finds attributed to the Etruscans, their highly decorated mirrors most mesmerize scholars. And the concept of "the mirror" as a philosophical idea was

One of the most important principles of Etruscan religion is the concept of the mirror as a symbol of the ordered cosmos.

central to Etruscan myth and religion.

The Etruscans were the pre-Roman inhabitants of the area north of the city of Rome, known to the Latin-speaking tribes as Etruria. As a people, the Etruscans were influenced by Greek colonists in Italy who along with their Hellenic ways brought their myths and their temples. Much of the Etruscan pantheon is identical or at least very similar to that of the Greeks. The Etruscans combined their special interest in augury and oracular prophecy with their local gods and their adopted Greek counterparts. In doing so they created an amalgamated religion and then used it to actively influence the development of the Roman pantheon.

One of the most important principles of Etruscan religion is the concept of the mirror as a symbol of the ordered cosmos. For the Etruscans, mirrors revealed the existence of reflectional phenomena within the universe and

ETRUSCAN MIRRORS

the ordering of the elements. Mirrors were illustrative of the existence of worlds within worlds that were able to interact with and influence each other. A mirror's reflection was evidence of another world, and the mirror itself was a portal.

Mirror Images

T hanks to the heavy Etruscan influence on Roman myth and cult, it is possible to recognize some of the guiding principles of pre-Roman religion. One of the basic elements of Etruscan religion seen in Roman myth is the concept of the creation of the bi-gendered sexual state by means of combining the sexes. This reassembling of the primordial gynomorphic, divine element is made possible by the existence of natural portals or mirrors. These reflective surfaces grant mortals access to a re-established hermaphroditic existence.

The use of mirrors involves witches. Etruscans and Romans both recognized that one's reflection was a mere shadow of existence. And as a "shade," the human reflection was an inhabitant of the underworld. In this way, the mirror became a portal to the world of the shades, the world of Erebus. It is only logical then that the gods or demons (in Greek "daimones") of the underworld were associated with mirrors.

The mirror was a portal to the world of the shades, the world of Erebus.

One of the most ancient mirror myths concerned with the regeneration of the hermaphrodite was the story of Narcissus. According to the Roman love poet Ovid, Narcissus was a beautiful boy who spurned the advances of any and all suitors, including both mortals and immortals. One of his spurned lovers invoked the goddess Nemesis, who punished the youthful Narcissus with the curse of falling in love with the one person he could not attain...himself.

> Shades were not "souls" but the insubstantial essences of human existence.

Self-Captivated

In Ovid's version of this heavily Etruscan myth, Narcissus becomes so enthralled with his own reflection in a pool of water that he can't pull himself away and even believes that the image is not his own: "While he longs to satiate his thirst, another craving grows within him. While he drinks, he is utterly taken in by the phantom form he has seen. He covets an empty hope and thinks that the reflected shade he has seen is corporeal...unknowingly he desires himself."

Narcissus, whose name gives us the medical disorder known as narcissism, ultimately starved himself to death in front of the reflective pool. From his body, a daffodil grew. The Romans used the daffodil as a pain-killing drug and sexual stimulant. The "narc" root in the name narcissus is taken from the Greek root for "pain-numbing." The daffodil came to symbolize the rule of Aidoneus, the god of the underworld.

The image of Narcissus falling in love with his reflection displays Etruscan and Roman beliefs in the reflection as the dimensional completion of the sky vault of the heavens. Mirrors were important religious symbols in Italy because they formed the other half of the cosmic sphere of existence.

"Shades," the non-corporeal reflections of physical life, were considered the disembodied entities that fled the body upon death. They were not "souls" but the insubstantial essences of human existence. And their proper dwelling place was Erebus, where they breathed the dark matter of the underworld rather than the air of the earthly realm or the ether of Olympus. The mirror's reflection was a reminder that another dimension existed where the shades of this life ended up—a place beyond the reach of light, where reality was a mere reflection of the physical universe of those who dwell in the light.

The myth of Narcissus was a warning to mortals who look to their reflection as a source of veneration. The "shade" is nothing to be venerated, in the mind of the ancient world. Self-fulfillment and self-worship were foreign concepts to classical civilization. The ultimate attainment of any Greco-Roman cult, including the mystery religions, was the recognition of the immortal forces of the universe, not self-advancement. Salvation as a means of spiritual augmentation was the product of Christianity and its bastard child gnosticism, not paganism.

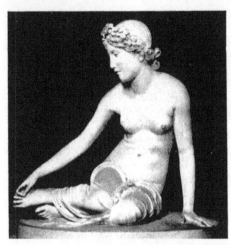

NYMPH SALMACIS

Merging with the Opposite

As learned from Narcissus, the mirror is a reflection of reality, not a source of venerable knowledge. And as a reflection, the mirror was the perfect place to find and restore the bi-gendered reality of existence. Hermaphroditic gods were not just primordial creative forces—they were also reflections of the primal state of all living entities.

Just as modern scientists embrace the biological reality that all living carriers of DNA have developed from sexless microorganisms, the ancient world believed human gender was not absolute but the product of a unified precursor. Looking into the Etruscan mirror was a means of rediscovering this reality. Seeing one's reflection was an act of discovery in which the viewer could call forth his bi-gender origins.

Another myth illustrates the re-creation of the hermaphroditic precursor to life through a mirror or reflective plane. Ovid, in his *Metamorphoses*, relates the story of the nymph Salmacis and the boy Hermaphroditus. Once again, the story is about the power of desire and human transformation.

According to Ovid, Hermaphroditus spurns the advances of Salmacis, a water naiad, who eventually just wraps herself around the poor boy after he strips down and dives into her reflective pool for a cool afternoon swim:

> "She embraces him while he fights, and steals kisses from her unwilling lover. She forces her hands upon him, strokes his chest without his consent...like a snake, she entwines him in her coils...both bodies are joined in one mass, and one face represents them both...their two-faced form could no longer be called singular or dual, nor could you say it was male or female; it was simultaneously neither and both."

As boy and girl come together, they merge into one being. And in becoming a bi-gender entity, Hermaphroditus is no longer either male or female. According to Ovid he is both and neither; he is actually three individuals: the male, the female and the combination of the two.

When Hermaphroditus submerged himself in the waters, he fused with his reflective opposite—the female nymph. In turn, the nymph received her own reflective opposite when she intertwined with the unwilling Hermaphroditus.

The imagery Ovid uses is that of a snake entwining itself around the formation of a conjoined couple. And this imagery is an intentional reference to the use of the snake as the animal that bonds with the bi-gendered creator gods like Phanes. Hermaphroditus doesn't realize it, but as he joins with Salmacis he is transformed into the primordial hermaphroditic form—the original manifestation of gender in the cosmos, the primordial element.

And Eros, or the god Desire, is once again the impulse that sparks transformative creation. For this reason, the gods of sexual desire are present in all three realms of the universe. They appear on Olympus, Earth, and even in Erebus. In fact, the myth of Persephone's abduction by Hades is itself a means of explaining the pervasive presence of erotic desire even in the underworld—where it may seem a bit out of place.

Hermaphroditus is actually three individuals: the male, the female and the combination of the two.

The catalyst of desire and its power to re-create the gynomorphic creator permeate all of Greco-Roman creation. The mystery religions popular during the rise of Christianity did not ignore this premise; and neither did the early Church fathers.

Nature provided the model for the gods. And in the minds of classical civilization and early Christianity, the natural model was that of the primordial hermaphrodite; the creator was a gynomorph.

11:

FROM BEAUTY TO FAITH

"Every intention of the King of the universe was enslaved by the young girl's divine breast."

—NONNOS

According to the culture that produced democracy, a hermaphroditic she-male created the universe. This god, known as a "gynomorph," an entity with a combined masculine-feminine form, was the key figure—called the "star"—in each of the mystery cults of the early Roman Empire. The gynomorph was the source of life; he-she was a font of purity, piety and wisdom for the mystery initiations that occupied the followers of Bacchus, Aphrodite, Isis, Mithras and Cybele.

The First Western Trinity

Christian priests, bishops and early Church fathers recognized the imposing power of the symbol of the gynomorph. Greek, Roman, Etruscan and Egyptian gods made popular by the Roman mystery cults relied upon this image of the creator-gynomorph to perpetuate their religions. The gods of the polytheistic pagans formed sets of sacred trinities, paired gods and goddesses with interrelated functions, who could be joined into a single, all-encompassing gynomorphic deity.

The classical, pre-Christian trinity was composed of a masculine, a feminine and a bi-gendered god. The god with both genders was called the "gynomorph" and was himself-herself the perfect combination of both the masculine and feminine divinities. The best example of this is the Zeus-Persephone-Dionysus trinity. Zeus, the masculine, seed-dispersing god, recognizing the perfect beauty and justice of the feminine goddess Persephone, joins himself with her. Their "union" or "yoking" produces the holy male-female entity called Dionysus, the divine gynomorph.

Modern scholars scrutinize myth through the lens of Christianity and in doing so are unable to understand the most basic aspects of Greek, Etruscan and Roman religion. Myth is not faith; it is not a doctrine or a set of truths demanding belief. Myth is a vehicle for poetic harmony, just as musical instruments are a means of producing melody.

Zeus was not the husband of Persephone, and Persephone was certainly not the mother of Dionysus. However, putting Christian faith and dogma aside, it becomes obvious that Zeus, Persephone and Dionysus are not people with bodies and marriages and children. As the Etruscans taught, the gods are realized through myth, and—unlike Jehovah and Jesus—do not

Myth is a vehicle for poetic harmony, just as musical instruments are a means of producing melody.

HADES &
PERSEPHONE

actually possess human characteristics. The Zeus-Persephone-Dionysus trinity only makes sense when it is viewed without the Christian cultural lens.

The Same and More

Hades and Zeus are the very same thing. Persephone and Semele are the very same thing. Dionysus is not just Dionysus, but Zagreus, Iacchos and Dionysus together, as a unity. Anytime post-classical scholars state that some mythical character was "the god of something," they have crossed over from paganism to Christianity. And this is why statements like those of the Greek philosopher Heracleitus seem so enigmatic. When he says that Hades and Dionysus are one, it is difficult for a culture so influenced by monotheism to understand his exact meaning.

Classical trinities, dating from archaic Greece, were numerous and probably reflect the earliest gods of Indo-European religion. Each trinity follows a single paradigm and culminates in a dominant triform divinity that embodies various unique trinities; this prevailing, archetypal triform god was the western world's oldest template for the divine trinity. These trinities were worshipped across the Mediterranean in temples, groves, caves, and underground chambers. For many years classical scholars have pondered the fact that classical temples traditionally house three gods; this mystery is explained in ancient myth when any three individual and distinct gods are combined into a single gynomorphic entity.

The gods Hecate, Selene, and Artemis came to-gether to form another trinity composed of masculine, feminine and bi-gendered elements. The summation or "joining" of Selene and Artemis formed Hecate. Cy-bele, Attis and Agdistis formed yet another unique trin-ity, whose individual elements were conjoined into a single gynomorphic whole. While there were numerous trinities like these in the ancient pre-Christian world, each was a reflection of a single primordial trinity com-posed of a queen, a king and a gynomorph.

Queen of Life and Death

n ature begins with a queen. Whether she is called Black Night, the matrix of the universe, Aphrodite-Urania, the primal source of life, or Mother Nature, the nourishing principle of generation and growth, the ancient world saw the origin of all biological life as a female, a cosmic queen.

The Greco-Roman pantheon is stuffed with primal queens. Hera was the great queen of the realm of ether, the ruling principle of Olympus. Rhea

The Greco-Roman pantheon is stuffed with primal queens.

was the queen mother of divinity, the womb of the gods. Aphrodite-Urania, known as Ishtar, Astarte and Isis outside of Greece, was the queen of the cosmos. And each of these goddess-queens was a member of a distinct trinity; each stood as a symbol for the primordial trinity.

These queens may have been distinct, but each pointed to a primordial queen whose power was the source from which they all drew their authority. In other words, each of the divine queens of the Greco-Roman religious world was a type of "The Queen." And this primordial queen, the oldest of the ancient polytheistic pantheons, was called "The Kore."

Eleusinian Mysteries

T he Greeks and Romans celebrated this primordial queen at the most prestigious religious festival of antiquity, known by the Greeks as the Eleusinian Mysteries. This annual mystery initiation took place just outside of Athens and reportedly culminated in the rising of "The Kore" from Erebus. Her appearance instilled the initiates with an understanding of the universe that was unique and coveted by the inhabitants of the Mediterranean world.

Persephone, the Kore celebrated at the Eleusinian Mysteries, was the prototypical Queen of the Greco-Roman trinity of triform gods. She encompassed all the powers of all the great queens of the gods, and was known as the author of life and death. Thus we find, in the Orphic *Hymn to Persephone*: "Persephone....venerated mate of Plouton...begetter of the Furies, queen of the underworld gods...mother of the roaring Good-Counselor who bears multiple physical forms...You bring to life and you kill all living things."

Persephone, the great female creator, was the feminine manifestation of the earliest western trinity. As such she was the initial creator and progenitor of everything living. Her divine beauty was the force of cosmic attraction that drove her union with the King of the primordial trinity, Hades, the Zeus-King of the underworld. And the generative outcome of their union was the great bi-gendered gynomorphic god known as Zagreus.

King of the Underworld

Western kings maintain order; and Hades, the primordial Zeus-King of Erebus, was no exception. As the mate of the generative Queen of the universe, it was Hades' exclusive right to maintain cosmic order. And of course, as the god with the great-

The primordial trinity is very much a story of romantic desire.

est knack for good-counsel, this primordial King joined himself to "The Kore" for one specific reason: to establish her divine justice—something the Greeks called "praxidike" or the practice of what is right.

In other words, Hades was great because he recognized the supreme beauty of "The Kore" and offered himself as her champion, as in the Orphic *Hymn to Plouton*:

> "Hades...you receive the shades of all living things
> and with death at your beckoning you rule all mor-
> tals. By your good-counsel, you joined yourself to
> the girl Persephone....Most holy ruler of men and
> gods, O Bacchic King, may you always be pleased
> with your servants who are devoted to justice and

respect for the gods."

In this way, the primordial trinity is very much a story of romantic desire. As a matter of fact, each of the

D ionysus is the bringer of Justice to the world of mortals.

Greco-Roman god-queens is presented as a "kore," a word that meant in Greek "a teenage girl in the blossom of life." That is, the Greek King-God had one very important job—the recognition of the divine right of beauty to rule the cosmos.

Much to the chagrin of the early church fathers who set the stage for modern western culture, the first judge of the universe was a teenage girl, not an adult man.

Bi-Gendered Gynomorph

A nd what about the third member of the western world's oldest trinity? What about the bi-gendered result of the union of the Queen of creation and her King? The classical answer is the Bacchic Lord, the underworld Dionysus, the crazed reveler whose sole purpose is the resurrection of "The Kore." The best illustration of this can be found in Orphic hymns to Dionysus, but there are many other ancient authors who taught the very same—Euripides' *Bacchae,* with its presentation of Dionysus' mother as the perfect burnt-offering, is perhaps the best example.

Again, modern classical scholars are genuinely puzzled by the inclusion of Dionysus in the Eleusinian Mystery initiation, but his place in the cult worship of "The Kore" is as old as any Greek myth, as we see in the Orphic *Hymn to Dionysus*: "I call upon roaring Dionysus, the bi-gendered primordial god, thrice born Bacchic Lord...Good-Counselor who manifests two physical forms, son of the holy union of Chthonian Zeus (Hades) and Persephone."

What scholars have failed to see in the texts is that Dionysus is the bi-gendered gynomorphic "offspring" of the union of the triform king and queen, and that he is responsible for the raising of "The Kore," his mother, from Erebus to the plane of the Earth realm. In other words, Dionysus is the bringer of Justice or "Praxidike" to the world of mortals. He brings salvation to humanity, but this salvation is not a creed, a set of commandments or a faith; it is a young girl in the bloom of life.

Beyond Personal Salvation

Thanks to the influence of Christianity, Judaism and Islam on the modern western world, modern scholars look at the Eleusinian Mysteries and their resurrection of "The Kore" as a means of personal salvation. Professors routinely teach that the cult practices at the great yearly initiation outside Athens endowed followers with a divine knowledge that ensured some sort of temporal salvation—something akin to the promise of eternal life given to Christians by their Messiah.

The focus of the Eleusinian Mysteries was the return of Justice to the Earth realm.

Unfortunately, this runs contrary to the poetry of

the mythographers who captured the essence of the
Eleusinian Mysteries and passed the main points on to
posterity in the form of songs. The Eleusinian Mysteries, with their queen-king-gynomorph trinity, were not
concerned with eternal life. The focus of the rites was
the return of Justice to the Earth realm; and this cosmic
justice took the form of a teenage girl whose beauty captured the gaze of all aspects of cosmic divinity.

The first western trinity was not a means to an end;
the primordial triform god was not a messenger of salvation. The earliest western trinity, as evidenced throughout the Mediterranean world, was a vehicle of Beauty.
The great queen was the voice and appearance of the
beauty of creation. In the face of the blooming Kore,
the Greeks and Romans saw a template for Justice.
They saw a means of establishing and maintaining a fair
society on Earth, not in Heaven.

This view was challenged by the Christians, whose
teachings countered the pagan world by asserting that
Justice and Beauty were not directly related and that
the manifestation of Justice was strictly a heavenly
prospect—not something that could ever be manifested
by mortals. In this way, the early Christians actively
reconstructed the primordial trinity in a way that
retained the female generative principle of "The Kore"
or "The Virgin" while forcefully turning their initiates'
attention away from Beauty as the rule of life to the
rise of dogmatic salvation. Faith, as a religious concept,
was a unique invention of the early Christian church in
response to the non-Christian world's awe and veneration of Nature's Beauty. Faith, as an instrument of the
Church, was used to shift the focus of western religion

12:

SODOMIZING THE LADY-BOY

"Your bi-formed Dionysus has more than just two manifestations…he readily transforms into numerous venomous shapes."

—FIRMICUS MATERNUS
(CHRISTIAN SCHOLAR)

The pagan trinity was composed of a divine queen, a king and a bi-gendered combination of the two known as the gynomorph. This triform god is evidence of the earliest form of western worship. The many and varied triads worshipped by Greeks, Etruscans and Romans were all offshoots of this queen-king-gynomorph template. Each of the pagan mystery cults prominent during the rise of Christianity relied upon this paradigmatic, ancient trinity. Christian leaders adopted the pagan triune model of god and reoriented it to best suit their exclusively male priesthoods. On a practical level the results were brutal and horrific.

The Queen's Majesty

The Queen of the pagan trinity was the highest object of adoration for non-Christians. When pagans celebrated their mystery initiations, like those of Isis, Cybele, Dionysus and Persephone, they did so with the goal of venerating the queen. The king and the gynomorph were both in positions to reflect exclusively upon the majesty of the queen. The divine king brought recognition to the universe of the reality that the queen was the guiding elemental principle of life. The gynomorph, in turn, served the trinity by actually bringing the queen into the world of mortals.

The bi-gendered entity became the savior of the universe.

The queen, or Kore, was worshipped for her manifestation of the "bloom" of cosmic beauty. Her beauty was the origin of justice in the universe. When the pagan Queen was joined with the King, the product or "offspring" of their union was a bi-gendered entity who became the savior of the universe through his selfless act of descending to the underworld—in death—in order to bring the divine Queen of life to the realm of mortals.

As Christianity developed, it recognized the enormous popularity of the pagan trinity and began to reshape the paradigm to support a mono-gendered religious model in which masculine sexuality dominated femininity on all religious fronts.

Using the religious machinery already present in Mediterranean society, the early Christians engineered a new trinity in which the gynomorph was the savior of humanity rather than the divine Queen. This resurrected gynomorph brought a new-born humanity into existence by the ultimate act of self-transformation.

Like the pagan gynomorph, Christianity's divine son conquered death; unlike the pagan gynomorph, Christianity's divine son brought salvation by refocusing the attention of masculine sexuality....by purging the feminine bloom from the eyes of the divine King.

Elemental Switch

The earliest pagan gods were bi-gendered elemental deities like Phanes and Eros, whose powers of attraction brought about the combinations of elements to form the universe. In this way, these primordial gods were very much the sexual elements present in the cradle of the cosmos that made all of life possible. Their ability to attract each other was the guiding principle of physical generation, as in the Orphic *Theogony*:

> *"Originally there was Hydros (Water), he [Orpheus] says, and Mud, from which Ge (the Earth) solidified: he posits these two as first principles, water and earth... the third principle after the two was engendered by these...was a Serpent (Drakon)...and its name was Khronos (Unaging Time)...Khronos (Time) generated an egg...it is from these that the third Intelligible triad is produced [Protogonos-Phanes]."*

The adoption and transformation of the pagan triform divinity was beautifully illustrated in great detail by Firmicus Maternus, a Christian scholar of the era of Constantine. In order to

The world we see with our eyes was created by a divine coupling of the elements with the Word.

modify the sexual paradigm of the pagan King-Queen-Gynomorph trinity, Maternus in *De Errore* shows us that the Christians first altered the primal elements of the cosmos: "The pagans are in error if they think they can assign supreme deity to a single element...the world we see with our eyes was created by a divine coupling of the elements with the Word."

Early Christianity, according to Maternus, taught that the cosmic elements were joined in the individual of the trinity known as "the Word." In this way the Christian Son of God, or "Word," assumed the role of the gynomorphic, primal creator, who, breaking with tradition, was uniquely independent of both feminine deity and the pagan "snake" of creation that symbolized the joining of the masculine and feminine genders into a single creative entity. And, of course, early Christians were proud of their independence from Nature's cosmic, elemental, generative snake...a symbol Jesus himself stepped upon publicly when he was in the Garden of Gethsemane with the naked boy. (See Chapter 15.)

The early Church promoted a vision of an elemental creator who engaged in sexual acts exclusively with the masculine gender.

The Christian act of creation by the gynomorphic member of the trinity known as "the Word" was important as early as the ministry of Paul the Apostle. And from its first appearance in the New Testament, the creative act of the gynomorphic Messiah was simultaneously explicitly sexual and exclusively masculine, as in *Colossians*: "By Him were created (ktizo) all things in the heavens and upon the earth...all things by Him and for him have been created (ktizo)."

Paul, praised by modern theologians and ministers for his exquisite knowledge of Greek, uses the verb "ktizo" to express the "generation" of the cosmos at the hands of the Word. But "ktizo" is a Greek verb that is used in sexually explicit contexts to connote the powers of sexual generation. A good example of this can be found in Aeschylus' *Suppliants*, where the father of gods and men is depicted as spreading good fortune by overseeing the "seeds" or semen of human families.

Paul used a specific word that reflects the male action of spreading semen to convey the image of Jesus creating the elements of the universe, but, in a shocking reversal of the pagan paradigm, Jesus wasn't portrayed as inseminating the female principle, but as a male-exclusive copulative entity. In this way, Jesus was exactly like his predecessor Dionysus, the resurrected pagan god who swore that upon returning from the underworld he would permit his servant to sodomize him. Paul, Maternus and the early Church promoted a vision of an elemental creator who engaged in sexual acts exclusively with the masculine gender.

Sexual Conversion

T he highly sexualized imagery of Jesus as the creator of the elements was exclusively masculine in nature. However, the early Church fathers, in conformity with Jesus' modeled involvement with the naked boy in the Garden of Gethsemane, focused their sexual rites of re-birth and creation on young, pre-pubertal

DIONYSUS

boys. In one of history's most stunning monotheistic revolutions, Christian leaders of the early Church used the pagan triform model of divinity to establish pre-pubertal, lady-boy gynomorphs as the preferred sexual objects of their clergy. And they taught—in an effort to combat the notions of sexuality advanced in Greek myth—that pre-pubertal boys needed to be sexually brutalized in order to be born-again.

The pagan world looked on the myth of Dionysus bringing "The Kore" from the underworld as a celebration of the arrival of Justice and the veneration of the natural trinity that ruled the cosmos. Firmicus Maternus reveals that the early Christians took offense at the figures of Dionysus and Persephone and instituted their own rites meant to correct the devil-inspired teachings of pagan priests and priestesses.

Maternus, an educated scholar, was well familiar with Greco-Roman myth. He even showcased his understanding of the Hades-

Maternus believed that effeminate behavior and open homosexuality merited execution.

Persephone-Dionysus tri-form divinity by referring to Dionysus as "Liber" and Persephone as "Libera." In one passage of his *De Errore*, he betrayed considerable disdain for the distinctly bisexual nature of Dionysus:

Specialist priests brutally raped young boys to "purge" them of the taint of pollution suffered in those swayed by sexual desire for women.

> *"The pagan school teachers prattle on that Diony-*
> *sus-Zagreus, this woman-shaped sexual object of*
> *men, engaged in deplorable sexual activity with his*
> *Greek lovers."*

Maternus claimed that the bi-gendered Dionysus had special powers over female sexuality and used drugs to charm women into performing sexual acts. In addition, Maternus openly supported the prospect of using capital punishment as a form of persecuting the followers of Dionysus and Persephone. In short, he believed that effeminate behavior and open homosexuality merited execution.

Dionysus and his followers may have meriteexecution in the eyes of the early Christians, but the Christians openly taught that young pagan boys could be saved through brutal acts of "purification."

Punishing Demons

Firmicus Maternus was no fan of the cults of Dionysus or Persephone, and he supported a special remedy for any promotion of the "devilish" concept of the bisexual divinity: he endorsed a form of spiritual cleansing that was gruesomely sadistic in its treatment of—of all things—children.

Bearing in mind that Dionysus-Zagreus—the offspring of the triform King-Queen union—was portrayed in myth as a young, pre-pubertal boy, Maternus supported popular rites of exorcists, specialist priests who brutally raped young boys in an effort to "purge" them of the taint of pollution suffered in those swayed by sexual desire for women.

Maternus, like many early church fathers including Tertullian, Minucius Felix and Cyprian, acknowledged that Christian exorcists used whips, incantations and "burnings" to chase the pagan gods out of boys. After all, these gods—like Dionysus—brought feelings of sexual promiscuity, and the only way to cleanse young boys was with the drastic practices of exorcists.

Maternus discusses the proper treatment of pagans who have been "possessed" during oracular performances. He recommends that the possessed boys have their "demons" beaten and violated out of them. The Greeks used young, unmolested boys in certain oracular procedures. They claimed that these same boys could never be sexually violated or they would lose their ability to be possessed by the gods in necromantic rituals like those conducted in celebration of Dionysus and Persephone. Mater-nus recommended applying the "fires of temptation," or

Maternus recommended sodomizing boys to drive out their demons.

the process of sodomizing the boys, in order to drive out their demons.

Demon-possessed boys who performed necromantic rituals in pagan mystery religions became the special objects of abuse by early Christian priests. Maternus argued that possession by gods like Serapis—another derivation of Dionysus—deserved the special ire of Christians and could only be punished by brutal physical torture. After all, the early Christians believed that demon possession was a harsh reality of the pagan world and required an equally harsh form of correction to rid the world of its corruptive influence.

In the face of paganism's outright veneration of post-pubertal femininity as the cosmic standard of justice, Christianity's leadership of the first few centuries of the Common Era adhered to male-dominant, Jewish traditions while distinguishing its own mystery rites from those of religious competitors by creating a new, brutal sexual ideal. The Christian trinity was an adaptation of the pagan triform king-queen-gynomorph model of divinity. By de-throning the divine queen as the bearer of justice, the Christian world perpetuated a model of self-rebirth in which a dual-gendered Messiah promoted the brutal rape of young boys.

13:

CHURCH SEXUALITY

"The King longs for your virgin beauty."

—ST. JEROME

The idea that the creator was a bi-gendered deity was a widespread belief of the Roman Empire during the rise of Christianity. The notion of the existence of gods with both sexes was so prevalent in the Mediterranean that early Church fathers were eventually forced to concede that their own creator-god possessed similar bi-gendered traits. Early Christianity used the image of the gynomorph, a masculine god with feminine creative capacity, in order to promote its own unique view of sexuality.

Jerome's Views

St. Jerome was an incredibly influential church father, who set the Christian world's moral compass on human sexuality. Known for his ascetic approach to the human body and its various appetites, Jerome flourished in the late 4th century and wrote extensively on sexual mores and the spiritual blessings of virginity.

Using Paul the Apostle as his model, Jerome set in stone the views of the early Church on sexuality. His tenets were basic and universal. He argued that sexual intercourse was a tool of the Devil meant to corrupt believers. Jerome thought the source of the moral taint of intercourse

Jerome taught that virginity was the highest moral good and that marriage was a necessary evil.

could be found in the first woman, Eve. He believed Eve brought sin into the world by means of sexual activity and that Jesus, who remained a virgin and was conceived without sexual intercourse, was the antidote to original sin.

Jerome taught that virginity was the highest moral good and that marriage was a necessary evil for the Christian pilgrim. In his *Letters*, a set of his own personal correspondence with various people, he repeatedly associates the loss of virginity with spiritual corruption: "I'll say what needs to be said: although God can do all things, He cannot redeem the virgin girl who has fallen. He is willing to free the one whom she corrupts, but He will not crown the one who corrupts."

Jerome placed great emphasis on the feminine origin of original sin, and refused to apply the same blame to men. His view was crystal clear: female sexuality is a corrosive spiritual influence and beyond redemption.

Jerome famously converted at an age after he had already begun to live riotously and with great license in the company of fellow students. This sexual freedom of his youth troubled him for the rest of his life after his conversion to Christianity. He frequently mourned his loose living and found himself in a constant struggle

The sexual freedom of his youth troubled Jerome for the rest of his life after his conversion to Christianity. against his natural physical desires. He explains in his *Letters* that his solution to this sexual dilemma was spiritual: "Destitute of any form of aid, I used to throw myself on the feet of Jesus, moistening them with my tears and wiping them with my hair."

Like many Christians of his day, St. Jerome felt a genuine disgust for human sexuality and associated physical pleasure with spiritual corruption. His views were based in New Testament texts and a reaction to the popular mystery religions competing with the early Church.

Mortified Loins

St. Jerome believed sexual intercourse was ungodly. Unlike many ancient, medieval, and modern Christians, Jerome did not view sex as a sacred act hallowed for a man and a woman who had entered into holy matrimony. Instead, he taught that the act of copulation was akin to demon possession and was nothing less than a tool of the devil.

Early Christians had witnessed the prominence of sexuality in the mystery celebrations of all the major Greco-Roman and Egyptian cults of the first, second and third centuries. The devotees of Isis, Cybele, Bacchus and Aphrodite inextricably conjoined religion and sexual intercourse. Jerome's views on sexuality are a combination of his devotion to Paul and a visceral reaction to the traditional activities of these mystery cults.

Jerome encouraged his followers to flee from inhaling the lust-inducing smoke from the altars of the pagan mystery religions. He rightly believed the wines that the mystery priesthoods mixed with drugs acted to promote sexual urges. And he believed the Roman gods, which he calls demons, delighted in the "burning" of sexual desire in their religious acolytes. He even taught that sexual urges were the source of universal sin: "All the Devil's power over men is in their groin; his courageous plot is centered in the generative organ of the woman."

The Evil Vagina

In other words, the early Christians followed clergy who actively taught that masculine sexuality was a form of temptation from righteousness that had its cosmic source in the female vagina. Women were the servants of the Devil, and men were their unfortunate victims.

The very thought of sexual intercourse was anathema for many of the early Christians.

In one strange passage of a famous personal letter on virginity, Jerome even wrote that male erections were subdued or mollified by God. Jerome forms a unique but lasting impression of God as sympathetic with the male sexual plight: women are a curse and their sensuality is the source of original sin.

The very thought of sexual intercourse was anathema for many of the early Christians. Jerome was among the most vocal ancient Christian sources on sexuality, but he was not the only member of the clergy to condemn the act of intercourse.

And Jerome didn't find intercourse alone to be ruinous. He was also one of the first Christians to link sexual promiscuity with contraception:

> "It disturbs me to enumerate how many virgins are deflowered on a daily basis; how many women are stripped from the bosom of Mother Church…some of these women make themselves sterile, committing homicide before the baby is born; many of them, when they perceive that they are pregnant from illicit criminal activity, take abortion inducing drugs."

It's fair to say that the early Church focused much of its sexual angst on women and denigrated the value of gynecological advancement. Understanding these views allows historians a glimpse into the unique sexual mores of the early Christian priesthood.

Desiring Youth's Bloom

In their efforts to explain female sexuality as a tool of the Devil, the earliest Church fathers painted themselves into a logical corner. Defining femininity as something evil forced them either to justify the purity of masculinity or to condemn gender altogether. The latter option was abandoned in favor of the former, based on the prevailing belief that Jehovah's creation of Adam was an act of perfection. Although the Jewish god's creative acts were always considered perfect, in the case of Eve, early Church fathers like Jerome argued that her genesis brought sin into the mortal universe.

The real intellectual difficulty with the Christian view of sexuality was the long-established classical view that women were the universe's creative entities and that femininity brought about life. The early Christians flourished within a Greco-Roman cultural milieu that actively venerated the power of women as creators of biological life. And the Church could not refute the obvious generative capacity of women.

Was it possible to reconcile the diametrically opposed views of natural female generative capacity and women's sexuality as the source of cosmic evil with the veneration of Jehovah and his Messiah son? Yes, it was. The Roman model of the gynomorph provided a unique bridge for early Christians between their spiritual disdain for femininity and the prominent belief in the power of female creative capacity. The result was the creation of Jehovah and Jesus as the male-female, dual-gendered creator-gods.

Clement of Alexandria, Jerome and Ambrose were all prominent Church fathers who promoted a view of Jesus and God the father as gynomorphs. Under their direction, the traditional masculine god of the Jewish religion was morphed into a bi-gendered entity whose essence was said to contain the generative capacity of women and the masculine capacity for insemination. The Jehovah of these early

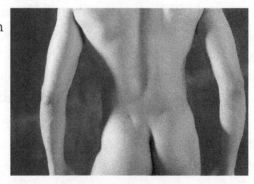

MASCULINE BEAUTY

The Messiah was consistently represented by the apostles and others as participating in a sexual union with the Church. Christian bishops is bi-gendered but clearly sexless. He encompasses the creative capacity of both genders but is completely asexual—in that he never engages in sexual activity.

Sexless Gynomorph

A sexless, bi-gendered, Jewish god may seem odd, but the real quandary of the gynomorphic Christian god was the hermaphroditic Son of God. Ambrose and Je-rome depict Jesus as the "nurse" of the Church, replete with milk-containing breasts and feminine reproduc-tive organs. The difficulty with a feminine Jesus lies in the fact that the Messiah was consistently represented by the apostles and others as participating in a sexual union with the Church, and his personal sexuality was therefore a serious consideration.

Early Christians considered Jesus simultaneously a virgin and a husband to the Church. They repeatedly used the image of Solomon's lover in the *Song of Solomon* to represent Jesus. However, the images of Jesus as simultane-ously a masculine inseminator and a feminine, nurse-like virgin were ostensibly in direct conflict with each other.

The resolution to this perceived image dilemma was the creation of virgin love, a special form of intimacy be-tween Jesus—a cosmic, gynomorphic, resurrection Mes-siah, cut from the same mold as Dionysus—and those

who renounced sexual intercourse. Unfortunately the
Christian leadership in Alexandria, with which Jerome
and Clement were directly involved, turned the object
of Christian sexual affection upon young, virgin boys.
Sexual purification rituals between men and boys became
prominent in Alexandria, and by the time of Jerome, the
Church readily acknowledged the problem that young
boys had become sexual objects for priests: "If you ever
feel a yearning for the bloom of young flesh....or are
struck by the idea of sexual play with fresh youth, take up
the shield of faith and quench the devil's fiery arrows."

Jerome recognized the conundrum of combining
concepts like the veneration of virginity, the concept of
the Messianic lover, and the idea that female sexuality
was the cosmic source of corruption. The logical outcome—the corner into which the priesthood painted
itself—was the idea that sex with pre-pubertal, virgin
boys was the only pure form of human intimacy; that is,
the sexual "purification" of children was God's will.

14:

HERMAPHRODITIC MESSIAH

"Physical desire is conquered by love of the spirit."
—JEROME

Christian priests deliberately reoriented the focus of contemporary masculine sexual interest from the classical model of the post-pubertal girl—known as the kore—to the pre-pubertal boy in order to meet the demands of their own theology. The Christian trinity was heavily influenced by the age-old triform gods of the Greco-Roman pantheon. Early Church fathers, specifically those educated in classical religion and myth, actively incorporated into their own mystery the rites of the king-queen-gynomorph trinity that belonged to the cultural environment in which the Church evolved.

Foundations

The king-queen-gynomorph triform was the basis of mystery religions across the ancient Mediterranean. In Greece, it took the form of the Zeus-Aphrodite-Dionysus triform and the triune godhead of Hecate-Selene-

Artemis. In Sicily it became the Hades-Persephone-Dionysus triform. For the Orphics, there were many manifestations that included gynomorphic gods Phanes, Priapus, Eros, Sleep,

In early Christianity, God the son was transformed into the hermaphroditic Gynomorph.

Night and others. In Phrygia and Lydia, it was the basis for the triune godhead of the Cybele-Attis-Agdistis trinity. Even the Egyptian trinity of Osiris-Isis-Horus shares common roots with the infernal Greco-Roman triform divinity—"infernal" here referring to any underworld deity or religious rite.

Using this widespread model of divinity, early Christian intellectuals built their own traditions upon a triform scaffolding. God the father became the infernal King, God the son was transformed into the hermaphroditic Gynomorph, and the Church, filled with the divine spirit, assumed the role of resurrected, virginal bride.

Christian intellectuals used the very same sacred mystery vocabulary employed by the priesthood of the infernal triform divinities to describe their own three-form God. But they did so with caution, as we see in Jerome's *Letters*:

> "I implore you in the presence of God, Jesus Christ, and his elect angels, do not offer to public view the sacred vessels of the temple which only priests are permitted to see, lest any profane man should be able to become intimately familiar with you, a holy container."

MARY

Secrets Concealed

Just like the pagan keepers of mysteries, the Christians forbade their own initiates from revealing any secrets of their purification rites. However, the intellectually minded apologists of the Church exposed much of the sacred vocabulary employed during their initiations. For example, the Latin virga was a prominent instrument or "vessel" referred to in mystery celebrations. For Greeks and Romans, the virga was a gilded branch used by the Kore—infernal Queen—to open the mysteries of the underworld and to reveal the secrets of resurrection.

The virga became the symbol of the divine Kore and was considered to be the holy key to the mysteries. Christianity borrowed the notion of the sacred vessel of the virga and used the Jewish holy books to support its use theologically, as Jerome wrote:

> "The rod (virga) is the mother of the Lord, elemental, unmixed with impurity, free from taint and with no added generative seed, keeping with the image of God, able to produce offspring as a single entity."

Jerome presents the Christian virga as the person of Mary, just as the pagan virga was a symbol of Persephone. Both women were holy, teenage girls who gave birth to a resurrection divinity. Like Persephone, Mary was considered to be a manifestation of the elemental origin of the universe. Mary, like Isis, Cybele, Rhea and Aphrodite-Urania, was the source of all elemental life. And it was Mary's purified female form that her son was called to resurrect from the grave.

Additionally, it is certainly no coincidence that the Latin words virga and virgo (meaning virgin) are based on the same linguistic root. Jerome, Clement and Ambrose recognized that virginity was metaphorically an ancient holy vessel, a symbol capable of "containing" resurrected perfection.

Resurrect the Queen

In the king-queen-gynomorph triform, the offspring of the queen had one important duty. He was the member of the trinity who resurrected or summoned the queen from the underworld; his job was to bring his perfect mother, the Kore, to the Earth realm so she might establish justice and then ascend to Olympus in order to take her rightful place among the gods.

The Queen was variously represented as Semele, Ariadne and Eurydice by the Greeks, but her most prominent form was that of Persephone, or Proserpine in Latin. She was also known as Isis, Aphrodite-Urania and Astarte among the Phoenicians. She was celebrated as "The Kore" by the followers of Demeter in Athens

and its surrounding countryside. The Eleusinian Mysteries, the most popular mystery cult of the ancient world,
was established to commemorate Persephone's resurrection from the dead at
the hands of her divine
son, who was sometimes
called Iacchos, Zagreus
or even Dionysus. See-
ing Persephone rise
from the grave was the
culmination of the Eleusinian Mysteries.

> I praise marriage and the
> conjugal union, but
> only because they
> produce virgins.
> — JEROME

The Christians recognized that the Kore, as the prototypical resurrected Queen, was symbolized as a sacred
instrument or vessel; she was a container, or pitcher, and
she held within herself the waters of the sacred springs
of the Muses. She was the cosmic source of inspiration
about whom the Muses sang. In other words, the great
Kore was the center of all ancient religion. She was the
highest object of veneration, about whom the universe
itself spoke. She was the great expression of creation.
She was the sacred bloom, the creator of everything.

Kore and Virginity

Jerome used the symbol of the Kore as the sacred
vessel in explaining his own veneration of virginity:
"No sacred vessel made of gold or silver is so dear to our
God as the virginal body."

According to Jerome, God the father established
virginity as the ideal state of existence—as a sort of
state in which he could best use his servants. For the

classical world, the Kore herself was the highest expression of existence rather than her physical state. Church fathers like Jerome borrowed her virginal purity while discarding her role as cosmic creator.

DEMETER

Early Christians used the Kore's image in order to advance their own understanding of sexuality, but grossly de-emphasized her person and natural beauty. The Kore was venerable as a virgin and as a mother, not as a creator; she was worshipped for her state, not for her ability to reproduce, as Jerome clearly said: "I praise marriage and the conjugal union, but only because they produce virgins."

Whereas the Greeks worshipped Kore for her own creative perfect beauty, the Christians turned the focus from her person to her sexual state—to her virginity. In this way, they created in Mary an altered replica of the Kore, a virgin-mother who could be worshipped for her perpetual virginity rather than her prominent role as creator of the universe. In adapting the image of the

Kore to suit its theological needs, the early Christian Church successfully co-opted the centerpiece of ancient pagan religion and thus monopolized the figure of the virgin-mother.

The Role of Jesus

Jesus then became the member of the trinity whose task it was to redeem his mother by raising her from the dead. This redemption, again a modified form of the Greek resurrection of Persephone from the underworld, was both similar to and different from its pagan model. When Jesus brought his mother to the Heavens, he did so by breaking the bonds of original sin, and thus made possible the universal redemption of humanity; when he raised his mother, he raised the Church...his new-found, virgin bride. Jerome again:

> "The bride of Christ is an arc of testimony, gilded both inside and out, a guardian of the law of God... so just as there was nothing in the arc of the covenant except for the law of God, let there be no external thoughts in you."

With relative ease, the virgin-mother Mary took the place of Persephone. As Jerome elsewhere states, Mary took on the attributes of Persephone...at one point saying she was the pride of her mother and an only begotten daughter. In addition, Mary's function was even the same as Persephone's: upon release from the

In the Greco-Roman mind, resurrection was a glorification of gods, not mortals.

underworld, Persephone established justice throughout the cosmos as the Greek "Praxi-dike"—another term exclusive to

T he Christians introduced the idea that the divine Son was destined to marry his resurrected bride.

the celebration of mystery rites: the bearer of just rule for mortals and immortals alike. For the Greeks—and subsequently the Christians—the virgin became the vessel for the fulfillment of divine rule or law.

For Christians, the bride and virgin-mother of Jesus were declared righteous by the death and subsequent resurrection of the divine Son. This is exactly like the resurrection performed by Dionysus, with one exception: Dionysus didn't redeem humanity, but merely made visible the eternal bloom of the Kore; he resurrected his mother because she was worthy of display—like a great work of art—not because he saved her or humanity from condemnation. In the Greco-Roman mind, resurrection was a glorification of gods, not mortals.

In addition, the pagan resurrected virgin-mother model was altered by the Christians, who introduced the idea that the divine Son was destined to marry his resurrected bride. According to the pagan king-queen-gynomorph template established long before Christianity, the son was the foil for the mother's blossoming, not her groom. The divine metaphor was not sexual for the pagans. Christianity embraced the opposite: mother and son became bride and groom in an explicitly sexual union.

This incestuous imagery produced by the earliest Christians startled and puzzled the people of Rome. Some of the earliest accusations against the Christians claimed that their famous "agape" feasts were excuses for incestuous orgies. Many Romans believed and reportedly witnessed that Christian mothers brought their sons with them to their secretive festivals in order to engage in sexual intercourse

The Christian concept of "virginity" is the very first time the western world saw sexual inexperience as a form of purity and not a form of ignorance.

with them. The offspring of these unions were aborted and used as filler for the bread of the divine sacrament, a proposition that had some ancient precedent but also bothered contemporary Romans. Tertullian, 2nd -3rd century CE, in his *Apology*, aggressively defends specific charges leveled against Christians that entailed incest and the cannibalization of aborted fetuses. The Romans taught that Christians were adamantly opposed to abortions performed by pagans but encouraged their own female members to abort fetuses conceived in incestuous relationships.

Filled with God

Judeo-Christian theology with its concept of "original sin" was the impetus for the alterations of the long-established model of the classical triform god. The Christian world turned its emphasis from the natural bloom of creation to the sexual purity required to please the masculine side of Jehovah. In condemning sexuality as the vehicle of sin by which Eve corrupted Adam and the entire race of mortals, Christian teachings necessitated a new religious emphasis on virginity as the redemptive principle of the cosmos.

The relationship of early Christians with their triform deity was very much a reaction to the necessity of making virgins the morally and spiritually purified elements of the cosmos. This idea was entirely absent from Greek, Roman and Etruscan mythology, where natural beauty was the highest good; Persephone was the divine queen because of her natural beauty and perfection—before and after her sexual union to the god of Erebus. In fact, it is safe to say that the Christian concept of "virginity" is the very first time the western world saw sexual inexperience as a form of purity and not a form of ignorance.

When Christianity exploded onto the stage of

EVE THE GUILTY

history, it forever altered the West's definitions of gender and sexuality. Worshippers of Jesus and his followers
were not just acolytes; they were, said Jerome, sexual
partners with God himself:

> *"Finally, after throwing off the burden of this age,*
> *sit at the feet of the Lord and say: 'I found him*
> *whom my soul sought; I will hold Him and not let*
> *Him go.' And he will answer: 'My dove is my one*
> *and only; she is pure. She is the only child of her*
> *mother, she is the pride of the one who gave her*
> *birth.' She is in reality the heavenly Jerusalem."*

The resurrected virgin-mother of Christianity filled the
role of the pagan divine Queen, while de-emphasizing
the pagan goddess' traditional role as the bloom of
creation—the highest good of all the universe. Mary,
unlike Persephone, was no longer a sexual object de-
serving of allure and veneration. Christianity brilliantly
transferred the sexual bloom of the infernal queen to
the resurrected gynomorphic son. In this way, Jesus
became the exclusive sexual object of the Christian
religious universe.

15:

NAKED WITH JESUS

*"Do you dare reveal the Cotytian rites and the
secrets of unrestrained Love?"*

—HORACE

Christianity developed in the midst of numerous popular mystery cults—and competed with them. The cultural matrix of the Greco-Roman world gave birth to popular religious movements that involved the celebration of bi-gendered gods. The founders of Christianity created a sect of messianic Judaism that was unique, yet highly dependent upon the religious environment of the western Hellenistic world. Jesus and his disciples adopted many elements of the sacred imagery and sexual practices of contemporary ancient cults.

Necromantic Horror

One of the most interesting developments of early Christianity was its adaptation of Greek, Etruscan and Roman necromantic practices. Classical necromancers called upon the powers of underworld gods in order to resurrect the dead and to use these ghosts for the purposes of divination. This necromancy was steeped in sex, drugs and brutality.

The first Christians actively employed ritual sexual rites that were developed and perfected by the Greeks and Romans with whom they lived. These secretive mystery rites involved the use of sex drugs, orgiastic celebrations and religious imagery that predates the rise of the Church by roughly a thousand years.

One of the most sensational of the necromantic practices adopted by the founders of Christianity involved the use of young boys in a ritual designed to facilitate the resurrection of souls of the recently departed. Horace, a celebrated Roman poet of the first century BCE, composed numerous odes and epodes in Latin, several of which highlighted these practices among the Roman people. His fifth epode is the re-creation of a ceremony popular among the followers of the triform goddess Hecate.

A Graphic Picture

Horace paints a graphic picture of the torture of an unwilling hostage, held against his will by devotees of necromancy. In this poem a young boy pleads for his life while several women bind him, strip him naked and begin to prepare him for sacrifice: "After pleading with them (the necromancers) for his life with quivering lips, the boy abandoned hope and just stood there;

stripped of his childhood clothing; his naked flesh proclaimed that he had not yet even entered puberty."

Horace goes to great lengths to emphasize the youthful appearance of the boy and specifically relates to his
audience that the poor child is obviously an adolescent
of pre-pubertal age. With great horror, Horace describes
the inevitable morbid outcome of the ritual: the boy will
be killed in order to summon the dead.

Horace's use of highly specific terminology associated with mystery initiations is by no means subtle and is
meant to create a believable religious setting for the so-
phisticated Roman audience that read his poetry. Much
of the shock value of Horace's fifth epode depends upon
its cultic authenticity; the Roman world was frightened
by the poem's gruesome depiction of ancient necromancy
precisely because of its realism. And Romans didn't take
necromancers lightly: they prosecuted them for their
shocking behavior.

Horace designed his fifth epode to reflect genuine
necromantic rituals. He purposely used the image of
a young, helpless, sexually vulnerable boy as a model
for an initiatory victim or sacrifice. The tension of the
epode is height-
ened by the boy's
compromised posi-
tion; his binding,
nudity, and ritual
preparation are
horrific facets of

Romans didn't take necromancers lightly: they prosecuted them for their shocking behavior.

ancient necromantic operations. In addition, Horace
uses distinct drug imagery and images of aggressive,

irresistible sexuality that are unmistakable elements of ancient mystery cults. The boy's captors have placed him in a compromising position and intend to torture and abuse him for the sake of communion with the dead in what can best be described as a "resurrection ceremony."

Jesus and the Naked Boy

The use of a "sexual sacrifice" to raise the dead was a common religious theme in antiquity and was exclusively associated with necromantic rituals. The victim was typically forced to undergo a sexual operation culminating in some form of death—either actual or symbolic. This death attracted the souls or "shades"

of the underworld and could be used to summon them for the purposes of oracular consultation. Necromantic priestesses believed they could consult these ghosts in order to learn the future.

Necromancers were not the only ancient religious worshippers who used young boys for divination.

MARY MAGDALENE

Ancient sources are replete with references to practices like "hydromancy," an art in which young boys were specifically selected to act as go-betweens to the world of the dead: donning sacred

The pagan image of the boy-sacrifice even appears in the gospel of Mark.

linen wraps after ritual bathing, young boys were forced to stare into water sources while being subjected to potent, mind-altering botanicals—with the hope that they would be able to elicit prophetic visions from the reflective surface of the water.

The pagan image of the boy-sacrifice even appears in the gospel of Mark. Jesus' famous visit to the Garden of Gethsemane, in the 14th chapter, is packed with puzzling necromantic imagery: "A young man was following Him, wearing nothing but a linen sheet over his naked body; and they seized him. But he pulled free of the linen sheet and escaped naked."

Historians, Church members, and innumerable apologists from the early Church were unsuccessful in explaining the presence of this naked child with Jesus. The presence of a naked boy with Jesus, late at night in a park, has disturbed people for ages, and from the outset of Christianity has eluded a comfortable explanation.

Mystery Elements

Among the more obvious of the mystery elements incorporated in this Greek text of the gospel of Mark are the use of the linen sheet, the boy's specific age, his nudity, and the fact that the episode takes place near a

Like the necromancers of their day, Jesus and his disciples used a sacred burial ground as a base from which to make oracular pronouncements about the future.

burial ground. The Mount of Olives, where Gethsemane was located, was a traditional Jewish cemetery. Like the necromancers of their day, Jesus and his disciples used a sacred burial ground as a base from which to make oracular pronouncements about the future.

The boy's nudity, youth, the use of a linen sheet, and the graveyard setting are all aspects of Greco-Roman religious operations; they would have been commonly recognized in the ancient world as facets of necromancy. Based on the worrisome connection with such nefarious religious rites, the early Church spent considerable time and energy in explaining away the reasons for the naked child's presence with Jesus. However, the fact remains that the episode of Gethsemane is highly evocative of an ancient necromantic ritual.

Cross-Dressing Baptists

Using naked boys to resurrect the dead was not the only necromantic image employed by Jesus and his associates. For the modern world, water-immersing "baptists" have nothing to do with necromancers attempting to resurrect the dead, but in the ancient world the two were inseparable. And the world's first baptists weren't just necromancers; they were also avid cross-dressers.

Juvenal, a Roman satirist of the late first century CE, wrote about "baptists." The Thracians, a tribe of northern Greeks, celebrated their goddesses Cotyto and Bendis with ritual purifications that earned them their iconic name from the Greek term "baptizo" meaning "to submerge."

Early baptists ritually cleansed themselves with water in preparation for the worship of goddesses associated with gender-switching roles. Male followers of Cotyto and Bendis dressed themselves as women and participated in rituals that blurred the lines of gender identity. Juvenal alludes to all of this: "But by inversion of the normal custom, women do not cross their threshold and are sent packing: the altar of the goddess is open to males alone. 'Get away you impure women!' is their cry. 'No music girl with her horn pipes here.' Rites like these were celebrated by torchlight in secret by the Baptae, who used to exhaust Cecropian Cotyto."

John the Baptist was no stranger to the religious traditions of the ancient Mediterranean. His odd dress, diet and use of ritual water-purification followed long-standing Thracian traditions. John's strange behavior was very much in step with contemporary accounts of the worshippers of Cotyto and Bendis. Like John and the Galli of Phrygia, these worshippers were known for eccentric views that involved the use of

Early baptists ritually cleansed themselves with water in preparation for the worship of goddesses associated with gender-switching roles.

JOHN THE BAPTIST

non-traditional dress and habits.

Thracian baptists and priests known as Galli worshipped underworld divinities. Both groups betray the typical signs of necromantic worshippers. John's theological interest in preparing for the coming of a messianic figure is exactly in line with the activities of the self-castrating Galli and their cross-dressing Thracian baptist neighbors. Based on their many similarities, it's likely that John was also a cross-dresser. In fact, his famous leather waist-belt is suspiciously similar to the ornate belts characteristically used by women in the celebration of the goddess Aphrodite. Furthermore, John's aggressive approach to "purifying" the public is reminiscent of Hercules' efforts to clean up the crime-ridden highways and crossroads of the ancient world; and like the baptists, Hercules was worshipped as a cross-dresser.

Mary's Alabaster Dildo

naked boys and transvestitism aside, Jesus and his followers were involved in additional practices that may indicate necromantic interests. The most peculiar of these is Mary's use of a dildo-shaped vial containing sex drugs. In the gospel of Mark, Mary famously anoints—or rubs oil on—Jesus in the days preceding his arrest and crucifixion: "While He was in Bethany at the home of Simon the leper, and reclining at the table, there came a woman with an alabaster vial of very costly perfume of pure nard; and she broke the vial and poured it over His head."

Mark tells us the container used by Mary was called an "alabastron." He also says it contained "myron" or "nard." This is important because myron and nard are very specific Greek words used to represent families of common designer sex

JESUS AND A WOMAN

Pope Gregory I even criticized the fact that Mary used sex drugs to anoint Jesus.

drugs from antiquity. In fact, these very same sex drugs were directly associated with the practices of necromancers. Nard even appears in the fifth epode of Horace when the poet mentions the use of a sex drug by an old lecherous woman who was ridiculed by her neighbors for her blatant adultery. Horace's necromancer is even impressed with the old woman's ability to concoct such a potent drug:

> "Let the bitches who live in the Suburra bark at the adulterous old woman on the prowl...a comedic sight...a senile tramp who anoints herself with nard that even I couldn't make so strong."

The nard-containing alabastron of Mary became an object of scorn for the early Christians. In a famous homily, Pope Gregory I even criticized the fact that Mary used sex drugs to anoint Jesus. However, what was most embarrassing about this episode is the fact that the alabastron was an ancient medicated dildo, a commonly used device for vaginal and anal penetration.

In a sexually charged scene from the Greek comedic playwright Aristophanes' famous work Lysistrata, one of the lead female characters wielded an alabastron and even used the sex drugs it contained on stage.

A literal translation of the gospel passage makes it appear that Mary was rubbing the drug onto the dildo in order to prepare it for insertion.

Myrrhine, whose name is a play on the word "myron" (her name could be translated as "Lubricated"), teases her sexually aroused husband with delayed sexual gratification. Her husband, Cinesias ("Banger"), awaits intercourse with her, but is distracted by her burdensome preparations:

Myrrhine: Get up.

Cinesias: I've already got it up.

Myrr: Want some scent (sex oil)?

Cin: Apollo no, none for me.

Myrr: But I will, so help me Aphrodite, whether you like it or not.

Cin: Then let the scent flow! Lord Zeus!

Myrr: Hold out your hand. Take some and rub it in.

Cin: I really dislike this scent; it takes a long time warming up and it doesn't smell conjugal.

Myrr: Oh silly me, I brought the Rhodian scent.

Cin: It's fine! Let it go, you screwy woman.

Myrr: What are you babbling about?

Cin: Goddamn the man who first decocted scent!

Myrr: Here, try this tube (alabastron).

Cin: I've got one of my own! Now lie down, you witch, and don't bring me anything more.

The alabastron was a six-to-eight-inch-long, penis-shaped vessel. It famously served as a container for drugs applied to the vagina, penis and anus before intercourse. Not only does Aristophanes use the very same vocabulary found in the gospel of Mark for the sex drugs and this dildo-shaped container, but he also uses the same verbal root to indicate the act of applying the drugs.

Applying Sex Drugs

Nards were applied by first vigorously rubbing them onto the skin or any object—such as a sacred penis used by the followers of Priapus. This vigorous "rubbing" created a warming sensation that characterized the use of these sex drugs in both the medical and non-medical texts. And unsurprisingly, when Mary applied the drug to Jesus, she first prepared it by "rubbing it on the alabastron." Curiously, New Testament translators omit this detail and prefer to translate the Greek technical term for "rubbing" as "breaking." It makes little sense and is out of context for Mary to have broken the drug's container, but the fudging of the Greek is necessary. For a literal translation of the gospel passage—which matches ancient custom—makes it appear that Mary was rubbing the drug onto the dildo in order to prepare it for insertion.

Jesus' use of the dildo-shaped alabastron in Bethany re-surfaces in a mysterious letter attributed to Clement of Alexandria, found at the Mar Saba monastery in the Judean desert. The author of this letter rails against the

Carpocratians, a gnostic sect of Christians that developed in Alexandria, whose members embraced, among other pagan-influenced traditions, a disturbingly open sexuality. The Mar Saba letter refers to Carpocratians as "wandering stars," an expression used by Greeks and Romans to describe necromancers and necromantic deities. The letter also states that the Carpocratians delved into the deep things of Satan—as king of the underworld—and thus hurled themselves into the darkness of the netherworld. Of course, any ancient necromancer would agree that this was the exact goal of their religious rites.

The Mar Saba letter may help to explain the presence of the naked boy with Jesus in the Garden of Gethsemane as well as Mary's gift of the dildo-shaped alabastron.

A Missing Fragment

Most interestingly, the Mar Saba letter discusses a fragment of the gospel of Mark that was reportedly left out of the original gospel in order to keep uninitiated pagans from discovering details of the most intimate Christian mysteries. This supposed censored fragment of Mark mentions another of Jesus' visits to Bethany, where Jesus raised a young boy from the dead, after which the two then entered what appears to be a sexual relationship. The episode, translated by Morton Smith, is unmistakably necromantic:

"And they came into Bethany. And a certain woman whose brother had died was there. And, coming,
she prostrated herself before Jesus and said to him,
'Son of David, have mercy on me.' But the disciples
rebuked her. And Jesus, being angered, went off
with her into the garden where the tomb was, and
straightway a great cry was heard from the tomb.
And going near Jesus rolled away the stone from the
door of the tomb. And straightway, going in where
the youth was, he stretched forth his hand and raised
him, seizing his hand. But the youth, looking upon
him, loved him and began to beseech him that he
might be with him. And going out of the tomb they
came into the house of the youth, for he was rich.
And after six days Jesus told him what to do and in
the evening the youth came to him, wearing a linen cloth over his naked body. And he remained with him that night,

The ancient world was
entirely absorbed in an
understanding of deity as a
mixed-gender phenomenon.

for Jesus taught him the mystery of the kingdom of
God. And thence, arising, he returned to the other
side of the Jordan."

The garden-in-a-graveyard setting, the resurrection of
a young boy, the scream of ecstasy, the linen garments
and the initiatory atmosphere all betray the workings of
a classical necromantic ritual. Clement refutes the ex-

istence of other reportedly excerpted passages from the gospel of Mark that speak of naked men mixing with other naked men. The Bar Saba letter creates as many questions as it answers, but it is heavily necromantic and may help to explain the presence of the naked boy with Jesus in the Garden of Gethsemane as well as Mary's gift of the dildo-shaped alabastron.

Regardless of the Church's struggle to explain the use of sex drugs in the gospel of Mark, and regardless of the presence of a naked boy in the Garden of Gethsemane late at night with Jesus, and regardless of the necromantic transvestism of the baptists, it is difficult to come to specific historical conclusions about the activities of Jesus and his followers. The only thing that can be said for sure is that Jesus and his disciples employed symbols, devices and religious performances that were very much influenced by the mystery rites of contemporary pagans.

The ancient world was entirely absorbed in an understanding of deity as a mixed-gender phenomenon. The oldest gods were neither male nor female, but both sexes combined. The ancient gynomorph, a hermaphroditic resurrection god, was the model for the mystery religions that dominated the Mediterranean world at the time when Christianity came into existence. Jesus and his followers were very much a product of their religious environment; they built upon the sexually charged figure of the lady-boy savior to carve out their own religious niche. Christianity owes much of its history and origins to the classical worship of the hermaphroditic gods of western society.

16:

EPILOGUE

S ex, drugs and religion are unique wavelengths of experience that belong to a single existential spectrum. For thousands of years of recorded human history, the western world has recognized the patent similarities of religious ecstasy, orgasm, and drug-induced euphoria. Greeks and Romans, the founders of democracy, western law, and the scientific method, believed sexual intimacy was neither a simple form of recreation nor a sacred act of procreation; they believed sex was essentially a religious tool...a means of opening a gateway through which mortals could communicate with extra-dimensional beings.

Classical priestesses, prophets, witches and necromancers labored under the impression that drug-enhanced sexual performance was a means of evoking

divinity. When done properly, drug-induced orgasm was a method of conveyance, a vehicle for transporting the gods from their native realms to the Earth. Mythic witches were not old crones; they were girls in the bloom of puberty, whose power of attraction was nothing less than overwhelmingly captivating—something

PORTALS

so powerful as to be able to attract the most potent inseminating divinities themselves.

Early Christians embraced pagan views of religion and sexuality and actively incorporated them into their religion.

Virginal Attraction

Early Christians embraced pagan views of religion and sexuality and actively incorporated them into their own peculiar mystery religion. They had no difficulties believing that a virgin could attract a god. Like the Greeks and Romans, they believed the sacred virgin's mission was to enable an immortal savior figure to access the human realm. And just as the classical world viewed this savior as a hermaphroditic gynomorph whose role was the resurrection of the just, so the Christians viewed their Christ as the immaculately conceived, resurrected savior-god.

The object of ancient Mediterranean religion was the establishment or resurrection of Justice. Justice was a divine force, an entity portrayed by Greek poets as a teenage girl. Justice was the last of the gods to abandon greedy mortals—known in myth as the Generation of Iron for their unbending devotion to the acquisition of wealth. Like the other Olympians, Justice refused to live with mortals after she discovered that human law courts had been universally tainted with the influence of gold. The goal of ancient priestesses and oracles was to open an avenue whereby Justice—now in self-imposed exile—could be summoned once again to return to human society.

Calling For Justice

The only god capable of returning Justice to her rightful place—according to classical myth—was Dionysus. As a child of Zeus, the leader of the pagan pantheon, Dionysus carried a clear Olympian mandate; for Greeks and Romans, the Olympians hated greed and impiety above all else. They viewed mankind's drive for wealth and success as the manifestation of self-worship, a terminal disease of the human soul characterized by acts of hubris. Only a true son of Zeus could purge the material cosmos of the human stain of self-adoration. And as a son of the mortal woman Semele, whose life was offered as a burnt-sacrifice to the godhead of Zeus, Dionysus was in the perfect position to raise his muse-like mother from the depths of the underworld and thereby return the rule of Justice to the Earth.

Justice cannot survive as either a law-code or a religious doctrine. Statutes and orthodoxy are inherently corruptible.

Justice cannot survive as either a law-code or a religious doctrine. The classical world recognized that statutes and orthodoxy are inherently corruptible. The founders of democracy knew very well that wealth and resources could amend written laws to suit small minorities of power brokers; Solon based his democratic reforms on this very premise.

Classical civilization also understood that any religious creed was subject to manipulation by generations of those with majority access to goods and services. Despite this depressing reality, ancient clerics, philosophers and poets taught that Justice could always be found in an incorruptible place—the heart of a teenage girl in the midst of the bloom of puberty...currently under the influence of love.

Teenage Priestesses

This belief laid the foundation for the use of teenage oracular priestesses in antiquity. Members of the ancient world as prominent as Socrates and Alexander the Great relied upon the songs of young oracular maidens to decide questions of war, social policy and personal interests. Greeks, Romans and Etruscans put such incredible stock in young song-writing girls because they believed their understanding of Justice was divinely inspired and completely incorruptible.

It was for this reason that Dionysus was the champion of Justice; the god's greatest personal mission was the resurrection of his young mother from the underworld. Dionysus' mother was important because, as a young girl, or kore, she attracted the attention of the highest, most powerful god. Zeus was captivated by Semele precisely because of her perfect, just beauty. Her songs charmed the god-king of Olympus, and their union produced the god of ecstasy. Greeks and Romans believed the song of a young girl in love was the purest form of piety in the universe, and the vehicle of Justice.

Dionysus journeyed to the underworld to raise his mother, the greatest kore, from the realm of shadows to the world of light. Her resurrected voice became the source of cosmic Justice that would ultimately triumph over the Earth-born monster of self-worship. Classical mythic heroes made similar journeys to Erebus, including Odysseus and Aeneas. And in both of these cases, a young teenage prophetess was the guide.

Sexual Rites

T he sexual experience of the maiden-singer was the ancient catalyst for transporting ordinary mortals to realms beyond the material universe. Witches and priestesses preserved sexual rites that were meant to elevate a potential kore from the state of normal pubertal development to that of inspired, visionary ecstasy. Using snake venoms, poisonous botanicals and other natural pharmaceuticals, oracular priestesses wielded dildo-like applicators to induce sexual ecstasy—the original symbols of western medicine still worn by physicians today.

As mated pairs, like Odysseus and Circe, or Aeneas and the Cumaean Sibyl, heroes and priestesses entered a netherworld, where they claimed to find direction and guidance from the dark gods of Erebus—gods who were particularly invested in the enforcement of Justice.

It is no accident of history that the mysteries of the Kore were celebrated just a few miles away from Athens, the world's first democratic city.

In the underworld, Greek and Roman heroes always ended their extra-

dimensional jour-
neys at the feet of
the great Kore, the
queen of the dead.
This girl, named
Persephone by the
Greeks, Proserpine
by the Romans and
Phersipnei by the
Etruscans, was the
sole source of cosmic
Justice. Her return
to Earth was cel-
ebrated on a yearly
basis in the most
famous mystery reli-
gion of the ancient
world—the Eleusin-

VIRGIN MUSE

ian Mysteries. The Kore's incorruptible song, her divine
resurrection witnessed by initiates, marked the return of
Justice to humanity.

It is no accident of history that these mysteries of
the Kore were celebrated just a few miles away from the
world's first democratic city. Athenians assigned great
value to the songs and poetry of the young girls who
served as the oracular Muses of ancient civilization.
Athenian statesmen were not afraid of the sexuality
of young singers; they believed the bloom of life was
a source of natural Justice and a necessary object of
veneration.

It is also no accident of history that the Christian
church saw the activities of oracles and pagan witches
as a threat to the survival of their own doctrines. Early
Christianity was able to absorb specific elements of

pagan mystery religions, but openly condemned the practices of female priesthoods and the pagan concept of Justice as a maiden's song. Christianity co-opted the figure of the gynomorphic savior, but altered the image so that the son-of-god's resurrection-doctrine was the ultimate source of Justice; Christians purposely and purposefully defied the notion that Justice originated from a young girl's love-inspired voice. In dethroning the Kore, Christianity established a perpetual authoritative creed that would prevail as the predominant influence of western culture for nearly two thousand years. Christianity deliberately and with malice aforethought silenced the voice of the ancient Muse.

INDEX

A

Adonis, 21-22
Ambrose, 34
anus
    anal intercourse, 16,
      52-53
    anal application of drugs,
      16
Apollo, 24
Aphrodite
    as Astarte, 113, 139
    belt of, 154
    castration, 24-25
    hermaphrodites 101
    Mithra, 22
    Urania, 21-22, 62, 98-
      99, 139
Aphroditus, 22-23
Artemis, 113
Attis/Agdistis, 30-32, 35, 37,
    113

B

Baptists, 152-154
Bendis, 153
bloom, 9-10
Bona Dea, 65

C

castration, 24, 28-29
Christianity
    early development, 26

incest, 143-144
inspiration, 144
mystery religion, 15, 147
oracles, 167
Phrygians, 33-34
ritual sodomy, 126-127
sexuality, 19-20, 54
sodomy, 54
trinity, 120-121
church as lover, 47
Claudian, 91
cosmic elements 10-11
Cotyto, 153
Cybele, 14, 30-33, 36-37, 38,
    75-76, 119-120, 137

D

daimon-demons 14, 104, 126
desire, 10-11
democracy, 11
dildos, 63-73, 74, 76-79,
    80-81
Dionysus
    bi-gendered, 14, 125
    bringer of justice, 117
      164-165
    dildos, 65
    drugs, 87
    kore, 124
    mystery religion, 15,
      119-120
    necromancy, 75
    resurrection, 143
    Zagreus, 30, 112, 125
drugs, 31, 52, 61, 64-65, 74,
    76, 87-89, 125, 155-
    157, 158-159, 160,
    162-163

Dr. David Hillman earned a Ph.D. in Classics and M.S. in Bacteriology from the University of Wisconsin, where he studied the medicine and pharmacology of antiquity. *The London Times* described his research as "the last wild frontier of classical studies." Dr. Hillman's work, while firmly grounded in primary sources—the original documents of Church authorities and others—is highly controversial. It is research that many modern Church officials do not want known. His dissertation committee refused to pass him unless he removed material about the use of psychedelic drugs in antiquity; he later published the forbidden material in *The Chemical Muse*. Revelations in *Original Sin* were even more shocking, especially in light of the worldwide scandals involving pedophile Catholic priests and the higher Church authorities who have protected them and allowed child abuse to continue for years. As soon as the topic of *Original Sin* became known, Dr. Hillman's livelihood was threatened and he was told he would be blacklisted in his field of teaching. He nevertheless decided to let the truth be known and completed *Original Sin* under a threat to his ability to support himself and his children. Now with *Hermaphrodites, Gynomorphs and Jesus*, Dr. Hillman again reveals the shocking truth about the history of The Church. For more information about Dr. Hillman's work, visit his home at Ronin: roninpub.com/orisin.html <http://roninpub.com/orisin.html>

Printed in the USA
CPSIA information can be obtained
at www.ICGtesting.com
JSHW082209140824
68134JS00014B/511